my revision notes

AQA A-level

DESIGN AND TECHNOLOGY
FASHION AND TEXTILES

Kate Bush
Julie Drake

HODDER
EDUCATION
AN HACHETTE UK COMPANY

Although every effort has been made to ensure that website addresses are correct at time of going to press, Hodder Education cannot be held responsible for the content of any website mentioned in this book. It is sometimes possible to find a relocated web page by typing in the address of the home page for a website in the URL window of your browser.

Hachette UK's policy is to use papers that are natural, renewable and recyclable products and made from wood grown in well-managed forests and other controlled sources. The logging and manufacturing processes are expected to conform to the environmental regulations of the country of origin.

Orders: please contact Bookpoint Ltd, 130 Park Drive, Milton Park, Abingdon, Oxon OX14 4SE. Telephone: +44 (0)1235 827827. Fax: +44 (0)1235 400401. Email education@bookpoint.co.uk Lines are open from 9 a.m. to 5 p.m., Monday to Saturday, with a 24-hour message answering service. You can also order through our website: www.hoddereducation.co.uk

ISBN: 9781510449275

© Kate Bush and Julie Drake 2019

First published in 2019 by
Hodder Education,
An Hachette UK Company
Carmelite House
50 Victoria Embankment
London EC4Y 0DZ
www.hoddereducation.co.uk

Impression number 10 9 8 7 6 5 4 3 2

Year   2023 2022 2021 2020

Cover photo © Shutterstock/Dahabian

Illustrations by Integra Software Services Pvt. Ltd.

Typeset in India by Integra Software Services Pvt. Ltd.

Printed in India

A catalogue record for this title is available from the British Library.

Get the most from this book

Everyone has to decide their own revision strategy, but it is essential to review your work, learn key facts and test your understanding. These Revision Notes will help you to do that in a planned way, topic by topic. You can check your progress by ticking off each section as you revise.

Tick to track your progress

Use the revision planner on pages 4–7 to plan your revision, topic by topic. Tick each box when you have:
● revised and understood a topic
● tested yourself
● practised exam questions and gone online to check your answers and complete the quick quizzes.

You can also keep track of your revision by ticking off each topic heading in the book. You may find it helpful to add your own notes as you work through each topic.

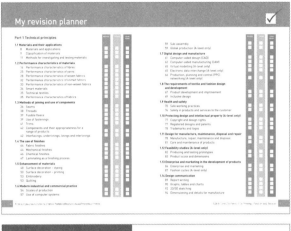

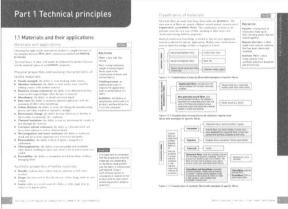

Features to help you succeed

Exam tips

Expert tips are given throughout the book to help you polish your exam technique in order to maximise your chances in the exam.

Typical mistakes

The authors identify the typical mistakes candidates make and explain how you can avoid them.

Now test yourself

These short, knowledge-based questions provide the first step in testing your learning. Answers are online.

Definitions and key words

Key terms from the specification are highlighted in bold throughout the book.

Exam practice

Practice exam questions are provided at the end of each part. Use them to consolidate your revision and practise your exam skills. Answers are online.

Online

Go online to try out the extra quick quizzes at **www.hoddereducation.co.uk/myrevisionnotes**

My revision planner

Now test yourself answers at **www.hoddereducation.co.uk/myrevisionnotes**

Exam practice

REVISED   TESTED   EXAM READY

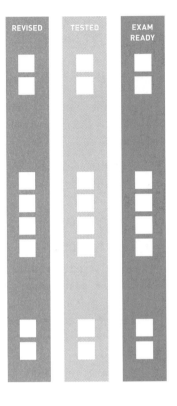

Answers and quick quizzes online at www.hoddereducation.co.uk/myrevisionnotes

Picture credits

All photos that have not been listed below have been kindly supplied by the author team.

Fig.1.2.3 © bennnn/stock.adobe.com; Fig.1.2.23 © Dontree/Shutterstock.com; Fig.1.3.7 © VPales/stock.adobe.com; Fig.1.4.2 © Sympatex; Fig.1.5.1 © Sirikorn Techatraibhop/Alamy Stock Photo; Fig.1.6.1 © Kadmy/stock.adobe.com; Fig.1.7.2 © Assyst Bullmer; Fig.1.7.4 © Teich/Agencja Fotograficzna Caro/Alamy Stock Photo; Fig.1.10.1 © bepsphoto/stock.adobe.com; Fig.1.11.2 © Martin Lee/Alamy Stock Photo; Figs.1.12.1, 1.12.2 & 1.13.1 supplied by Denise Davies; Fig.1.13.2 © Everett Collection Historical/Alamy Stock Photo; Fig.1.13.3 © Ulia Koltyrina/Stock.adobe.com; Fig.1.13.4 © Peter Atkins/Stock.adobe.com; Fig.1.13.5 © Armen Gharibyan/Alamy Stock Photo; Fig.1.14.1 supplied by Denise Davies; Fig.1.14.10 © oliver leedham/Alamy Stock Photo; page 97 © Liaurinko/stock.adobe.com; Fig.2.1.2 supplied by Amanda Dick; Fig.2.2.1 © Anton Oparin/123RF; Fig.2.2.2 © Photo Researchers/Science History Images/Alamy Stock Photo; Fig.2.2.3 © Christopher Stewart/Alamy Stock Photo; Fig.2.2.4 © Ukartpics/Alamy Stock Photo; Fig.2.2.5 © parkerphotography / Alamy Stock Photo; Fig.2.2.6 © Eileen Tweedy/REX/Shutterstock; Fig.2.2.7 © Lesia Pavlenko/123RF; Fig.2.2.8 © Chicago History Museum/Archive Photos/Getty Images; Fig.2.3.1 © Chronicle/Alamy Stock Photo; Fig.2.3.2 © Tomokoasano/123RF; Fig.2.3.3 © Vitaly tiagunov/stock.adobe.com; Fig.2.3.4 © Douglas Pollard/Conde Nast Collection/Getty Images; Fig.2.3.5 © By Archivist/Stock.adobe.com; Fig.2.3.6 © Pictorial Press/Pictorial Press Ltd/Alamy Stock Photo; Fig.2.3.7 © George Chinsee/Thomas Iannaccone/Penske Media/REX/Shutterstock; Fig.2.3.8 © Iamnee/Adobe.stock.com; Fig.2.3.9 © Fairtrade International; Fig.2.4.3 supplied by Amanda Dick; Fig.2.5.1 © xPACIFICA/Alamy Stock Photo; Fig.2.9.1 © Elenovsky/Shutterstock.com; Fig.2.9.2 © Harris Tweed Authority, www.harristweed.org; Fig.2.9.3 © Global Organic Textile Standard; Fig.2.10.1 © MigrenArt/stock.adobe.com; Fig.2.10.2 © Adrian davies/Alamy Stock Photo

Part 1 Technical principles

1.1 Materials and their applications

Materials and applications

Choosing the right textile materials for products is complex because of the interplay between **fibre**, **yarn**, construction method and **finishing processes**.

The final choice of fabric will mostly be influenced by product function and the material's physical and **aesthetic** properties.

Physical properties and working characteristics of textile materials

- **Tensile strength:** the ability to resist breaking under tension.
- **Abrasion resistance:** the ability to resist surface wear caused by rubbing contact with another material.
- **Elasticity (crease resistance):** the ability to be deformed and then return to the original shape when the force is removed.
- **Absorbency:** the ability to absorb and retain liquid.
- **Easy-care:** the ability to maintain optimum appearance with the minimum of effort when laundering.
- **Colour fastness:** the ability to retain dye during the manufacturing process and when washed or exposed to sunlight.
- **Electrostatic charge:** the ability for static electricity to develop in fibres under exceptionally dry conditions.
- **Thermal insulation:** the ability to trap air, preventing the transfer of heat through the material.
- **Corrosive solvent resistance:** the ability to withstand attack and decay from substances such as chlorine bleach.
- **Microorganism and insect resistance:** the ability to withstand attack and decay from organisms such as bacteria and moths.
- **Flammability:** the ability to burn or ignite, causing fire or combustion.
- **Thermoplasticity:** the ability to become pliable and mouldable when heated, enabling textures and creases to be set and retained once cooled.
- **Formability:** the ability to manipulate and deform fabrics without damaging them.

Aesthetic properties of textile materials

- **Handle:** evaluates how a fabric behaves, performs or feels when touched.
- **Drape:** the term used to describe the way a fabric hangs under its own weight.
- **Lustre:** refers to a textile material's ability to reflect light from its surface so it appears glossy.

Key terms

Fibre: a fine, hair-like thread.

Yarn: a long continuous length of twisted (spun) fibres used in the construction of woven and knitted fabrics.

Finishing process: an additional process to improve the appearance and/ or performance of a fabric.

Aesthetics: the beauty or tastefulness of the look of a product, and how attractive it is to the consumer.

Exam tip

It is important to remember that the properties of textile materials vary depending on the fibres used and the way the fabric is constructed and finished. Ensure each of these factors is considered in relation to the product and its users when answering product analysis questions.

Classification of materials

All textile fibres are made from long-chain molecules (**polymers**). The main sources of fibres are natural cellulose, natural protein, manufactured (**regenerated**) and **synthetic fibres**. The combination of atoms in the polymers varies for each type of fibre, resulting in fibres from each classification having different properties.

Material classification knowledge is needed so that the most appropriate material is selected for specific applications. Within some classifications a more in-depth knowledge of fibres is required at A-level.

Key terms

Polymer: a long chain of molecules made up of fibre-forming atoms that are linked together.

Regenerated fibre: a fibre made from natural cellulose that has been chemically modified.

Synthetic fibre: a fibre made entirely from synthetic polymers based on petrochemicals.

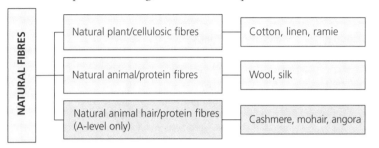

Figure 1.1.1 Classification of natural fibres with examples of specific fibres

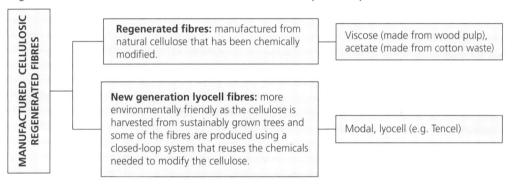

Figure 1.1.2 Classification of manufactured cellulosic regenerated fibres with examples of specific fibres

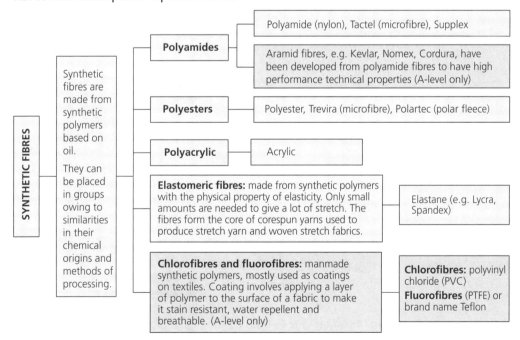

Figure 1.1.3 Classification of synthetic fibres with examples of specific fibres

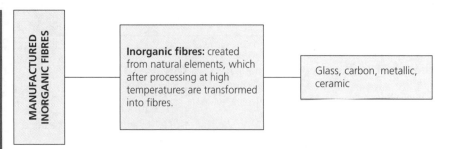

Figure 1.1.4 Classification of manufactured inorganic fibres with examples of specific fibres

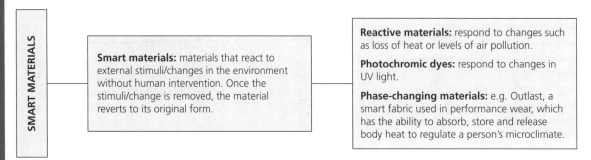

Figure 1.1.5 Classification of smart materials with examples of specific materials

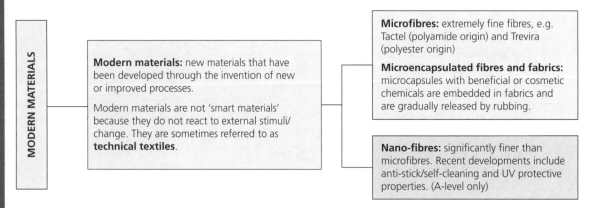

Figure 1.1.6 Classification of modern materials with examples of specific materials

Key terms

Natural fibre: a fibre that comes from a natural cellulose (plant) or protein (animal) source.

Smart material: a material that is able to react to external stimuli or changes in its environment without human intervention.

Modern material: a material that has been developed through the invention of new or improved processes.

Microfibre: an extremely fine synthetic fibre.

Microencapsulated fibre: a microfibre that has tiny capsules containing health or cosmetic chemicals embedded into its hollow centre.

Nano-fibre: an extremely lightweight strong fibre that is less than one micron in diameter.

Methods for investigating and testing materials

REVISED

Material testing

Material testing is used to help select the most appropriate fabric for a product. When setting up tests the process and parameters must be consistently fair.

20 cm
Wire marker
Paper fuse stapled to fastener
Light with match
Heat-proof surface

Figure 1.1.7 Workshop test for flammability

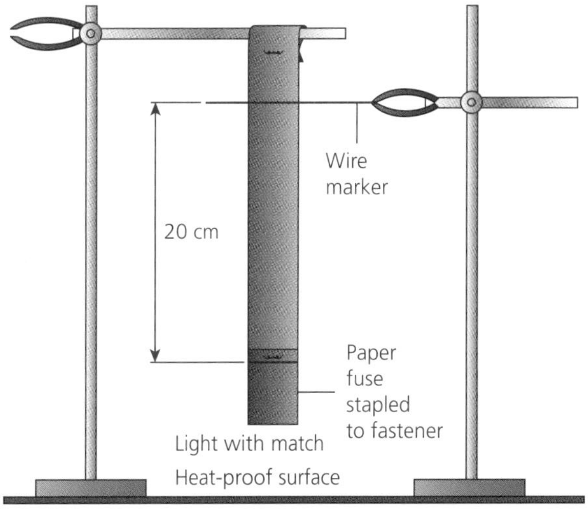

Simple workshop tests

Flammability

- Use precisely cut fabric samples and paper fuses.
- Light the fuse and use a stopwatch to time how long it takes for the flame to reach the wire marker.
- Record the time and other predetermined observations such as what happens when the flame comes into contact with the fabric.

Crease resistance

- The fabric is folded in half and placed between pieces of paper under the weight.
- After placing the fabric sample on the measuring block as shown in Figure 1.1.8, leave it to recover for five minutes then calculate the distance between its two ends on the horizontal scale.
- Record the result and repeat with other fabrics being tested.

4 cm
1.5 cm
5 min
kg
20 10 0 10 20

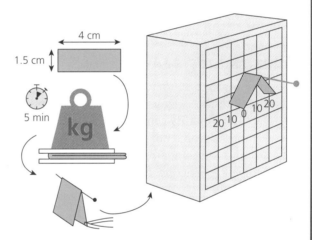

Figure 1.1.8 Workshop test for crease resistance

Shrink resistance

- Sew coloured cross-stitches or use a permanent pen to mark an exact 10 cm square.
- Retain a **control** sample and wash the remaining samples at different temperatures and levels of washing machine agitation.
- Dry and iron the samples.
- Work out the percentage shrinkage, for example:
  length between a and b before washing = 10 cm
  length between a and b after washing = 9.5 cm
  percentage shrinkage = distance before − distance after ÷ original length × 100

  $$10 - \frac{9.5}{10} \times 100 = 5\%$$

> **Key term**
>
> **Control:** a sample that is untreated or unchanged.

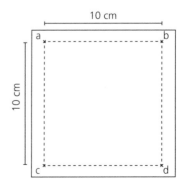

10 cm
10 cm
a
b
c
d

Figure 1.1.9 Workshop test for shrink resistance

Colour fastness

The most important factors affecting colour fastness are washing and exposure to sunlight.

- Workshop tests can replicate industrial tests for wash fastness. Samples are sewn onto white fabric and washed for a predetermined time at an agreed temperature. The dried samples are compared to a control sample and the white fabric is checked for staining.
- Reliable workshop testing for light fastness in fabrics is impossible. A prolonged period of time is needed and light intensity cannot be controlled in the same way as in a laboratory.

Strength

A test for fabric strength is also difficult to replicate in a workshop. It is impossible to achieve the large forces needed to break a fabric using basic tools and equipment. However, some observations can be recorded using a simple test.

- Prepare same-sized samples.
- Make a small cut at the warp, weft and bias edges.
- Tear the samples along the cut to see which tears easily and which fabric requires more force.

Pilling

Pilling is the formation of little balls of fibres (pills) on the surface of a fabric as a result of wear and friction. It occurs when weak fibres from blended staple yarns are pushed out and held on the surface by the stronger fibres. A simple abrasion test can be done to assess pilling.

- Fabric samples are stapled onto a wooden block.
- Glass paper is stapled onto a smaller wooden block.
- The glass paper block is rubbed over the surface of the fabric to simulate wear.
- The number of passes required for pills to start forming on the surface of the fabric is recorded.

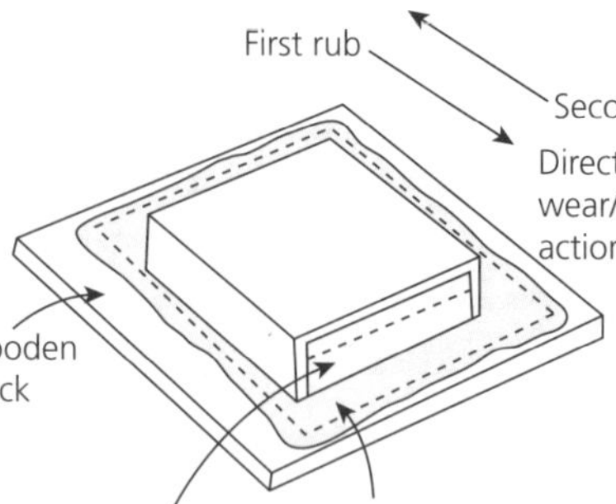

Figure 1.1.10 Workshop test for abrasion and pilling

Industrial tests (A-level only)

Industrial tests are an important way of ensuring a product complies with the designer's specifications, and include the manufacturer's **quality control** checks and **quality assurance** standards. For example, a product displaying a BSI Kitemark (see Chapter 1.9, page 76) gives an assurance to consumers that the product is safe and meets agreed product **performance codes**.

Industrial tests are usually carried out in laboratories in controlled conditions using specialist-testing machinery and standardised test pieces of materials.

Flammability

Industrial test 1: minimum flame application time to cause ignition

- The prepared fabric sample is held vertically in a metal frame.
- A small flame from a Bunsen burner is applied for two seconds, then three, four, six, eight and ten seconds until it catches fire.
- The test is complete if the fabric burns for more than one second.
- The time and any other predetermined observations are recorded.

Industrial test 2: flame spread and flame behaviour

- This test is used on fabrics that have low flammability.
- A small flame is applied to a prepared fabric sample and removed after ten seconds.
- The duration of the flame and afterglow are timed and any debris is recorded.
- The size of the hole burned into the fabric is measured and recorded.

> **Key terms**
>
> **Quality control (QC):** checking the product during the production run to test it against the specification.
>
> **Quality assurance (QA):** the planning of procedures and policies that ensure good-quality products.
>
> **Performance codes:** the technical requirements for a product, material or process to be fit for its intended purpose.

Industrial test 3: rate of flame spread

- A large sample of fabric is placed in a metal frame.
- Cotton trip threads, attached to timers, are placed horizontally.
- A small flame is applied and then removed after ten seconds.
- As each cotton trip thread is burnt through, its timer will stop, showing the burn distance and allowing the burning rate to be calculated.

Crease resistance

- Standard test pieces are cut from wrinkle-free fabric.
- Samples are kept in standard room conditions to ensure the fabric temperature and humidity is identical.
- A sample is folded in half and compressed under a load for a specified time.
- The load is removed and one end of the creased sample is clamped onto the instrument. The other end is allowed to fall free.
- The dial of the instrument is rotated to keep the free edge of the sample in line with the knife edge.
- At the end of the time allowed for recovery, the recovery angle is recorded from the engraved scale.
- The larger the angle of recovery the better the crease resistance.

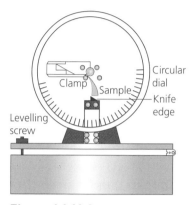

Figure 1.1.11 Crease recovery tester

Shrink resistance

- The fabric sample is overlocked to prevent fraying.
- Permanent ink is used to mark precise reference points on the fabric.
- The prepared fabric samples are washed with pieces of polyester fabric to replicate a normal wash load.
- The samples are dried using all available options.
- If the results of re-measuring between the reference points show a change has occurred, the formula used in the workshop test is applied to calculate the percentage change.
- Fabric shrinkage is shown as a negative percentage. Fabric stretch, as a result of the test, is shown as a positive percentage.

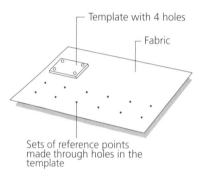

Figure 1.1.12 Using a template to mark reference points to assess shrinkage in fabrics

Colour fastness

Industrial test 1: wash fastness

- Samples are cut to an agreed size.
- Each sample is secured in a white fabric 'envelope' and washed for a set time at an agreed temperature.
- The dried samples are compared to the control sample. Changes in colour and the staining of the 'envelope' fabric are assessed using grey scales. The best grade is 5 and the worst grade is 1.

Industrial test 2: wash fastness

- Samples are cut to an agreed size.
- A **multi-fibre swatch** is sewn to the sample.

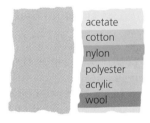

Figure 1.1.13 Multi-fibre swatch before and after colour fastness wash test

---

Key terms

Colour fastness: the ability of a fibre or fabric to retain dye fastness during manufacturing processes and when washed or exposed to sunlight.

Multi-fibre swatch: a narrow band of woven fabric containing separate segments of acetate, cotton, nylon, polyester, acrylic and wool fibres. It is used to demonstrate the uptake of dye staining when washing different types of fabric.

- Accelerated washing (replicates five or more home washes) is performed in canisters placed in a machine called a launderometer.
- **Grey scale cards** and the control sample are used to evaluate changes in shade, and the extent of the staining on different fibres is recorded.

Industrial test 3: light fastness

- Samples are cut to an agreed size.
- Two-thirds of each sample is enclosed in an opaque cover.
- The uncovered area of the sample is exposed to intense artificial light generated by a **Xenon arc lamp**. The light is filtered to replicate the accelerated intensity of natural daylight through glass.
- The area of the exposed sample is compared with the covered part using grey scale cards.

Strength

Strip test: tensile strength test for woven fabrics

- Rectangular fabric samples are cut in a direction parallel to the warp and weft.
- To ensure all yarns in the sample run along its entire length, the width of each sample is reduced to 5 cm by **raveling** (removing) yarn from both edges.
- The sample is stretched, and the distance travelled is plotted, giving information on extensibility, yield point, maximum load and final breaking point.
- The test is repeated with samples cut in the warp and weft directions.
- Non-woven fabrics are tested for strength in the same way using a strip of fabric that can be cut in any direction as non-woven fabrics have no straight grain.

Bursting test: strength test for knitted fabrics

- A circle of knitted fabric is clamped over a rubber diaphragm.
- Air or water is pumped under pressure into a chamber below the sample fabric and rubber diaphragm.
- The pressure is applied radially and is increased until the knitted fabric ruptures (bursts).
- The pressure needed to rupture the fabric is called its 'bursting strength'.

> **Key terms**
>
> **Grey scale cards:** used to show differences in colour intensity when comparing control samples with samples exposed to washing and UV light.
>
> **Xenon arc lamp:** produces a bright white light that closely mimics natural sunlight.
>
> **Raveled fabric:** fabric that has yarn teased or drawn out from its cut edges giving it a frayed appearance.

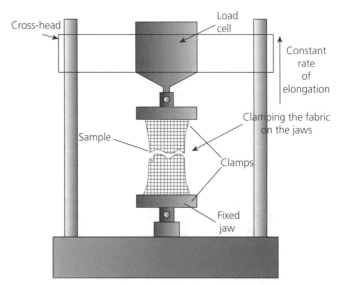

Figure 1.1.14 Industrial test for tensile strength

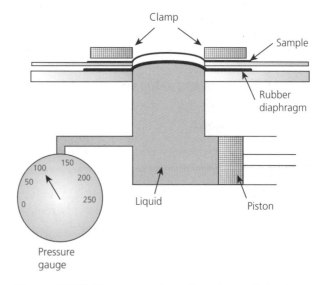

Figure 1.1.15 Diaphragm bursting strength tester

Pilling

A Martindale machine tests for abrasion and pilling.

- Circular samples of the test fabrics are clamped onto one of the machine's four discs and a weight is put onto each disc.
- The test samples are rubbed against an abrasive fabric.
- The machine controls and records the number of rubbing cycles.
- The test samples are examined at regular intervals for the presence of wear leading to pilling.
- On completion, the samples are compared, in a light box, with the control sample

> **Exam tip**
>
> Be able to state the purpose of named fabric tests and describe how each test is carried out fairly. List the differences between workshop and industrial tests.

> **Typical mistake**
>
> Don't describe an industrial testing method when a workshop testing method is asked for and remember to explain how the test results are interpreted.

Now test yourself

TESTED ☐

1 Place each fibre listed below in the correct column of the table. You should use each fibre once only.

Modal   Polartec   Linen   Silk
Acrylic   Ramie   Tencel   Tactel

Natural cellulose	Natural protein	Regenerated	Synthetic

2 Inorganic fibres are an example of which classification?
3 How do new generation lyocell fibres differ from regenerated fibres?
4 Define what is meant by the term 'smart material' and name two different smart materials.
5 Describe the key difference between simple workshop tests and industrial tests.
6 Explain how material tests can be made fair.
7 How is percentage shrinkage in a fabric calculated?
8 Use notes and diagrams to describe how a workshop test for pilling can be set up to mimic a Martindale machine.
9 Why are non-woven fabrics just cut and not raveled when preparing fabric samples for the tensile strength strip test?

1.2 Performance characteristics of materials

Performance characteristics of fibres

The properties of fibres vary according to their source, internal structure and physical shape.

Natural plant/cellulose fibres

Cotton

Cotton is the most widely used natural plant/cellulose fibre. It comes from the seed fibre found in the cotton bolls of the cotton plant.

> **Key terms**
>
> **Elasticity/extensibility:** the measure of how much a fabric will stretch and extend.
>
> **Handle:** how a fabric feels when touched.

Table 1.2.1 Properties/characteristics of cotton and its uses

Properties/characteristics	Examples	Uses
Naturally breathable, conducts heat away from the body. Very absorbent. Non-static as moisture is present. Good strength due to its natural twist. Very little **elasticity**, creases easily. Highly flammable. Poor insulator. Comfortable and soft **handle**. Damaged by mildew and prolonged sunlight exposure. Biodegradable.	Calico, terry towelling, muslin, flannel, voile, winceyette, chambray, poplin, denim, drill, gingham, madras, seersucker, corduroy, velvet, knitted jersey, velour	Apparel fabrics: shirts, dresses, jeans, underwear, socks, uniforms. Home textiles: towels, sheeting, curtains, soft furnishings, throws. Commercial textiles: medical dressings, nappies, sewing threads, ropes, filters. Leisure textiles: tents, awnings, boat sails, bags, sportswear. Blended and mixed, usually with polyester, wool and elastane.

Cotton fibre production (A-level only)

- Cotton grows in a boll around the seeds of cotton plants.
- Harvesting is carried out by hand or using a picking machine.
- The fibres are separated from the seeds using a process called ginning.
- Mechanical purification is used to remove foreign matter.
- The fibres are scoured to remove the natural wax coating from the surface of the fibres.
- The processed cotton fibres are spun into staple fibre yarns.

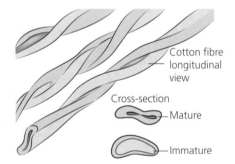

Figure 1.2.1 The structure of cotton fibres

Linen

Linen is one of the most expensive natural fibres. It is labour-intensive to produce so is produced in small quantities. Linen comes from the bast fibre of the flax plant stem.

Table 1.2.2 Properties/characteristics of linen and its uses

Properties/characteristics	Examples	Uses
Highly absorbent, naturally breathable. Very strong due to the longer length of the staple fibres. Poor elasticity, creases easily. Highly flammable. Poor insulator. Flat surface reflects light, so it has a subtle **lustre**. Poor **drape** and stiff handle. Damaged by mildew, sweat and bleach. Biodegradable.	Crash, duck, huckaback, interlining, Holland, union (half linen – fabric has cotton warp yarns and linen weft)	Apparel fabrics: summer or tropical garments. Home textiles: tablecloths, dish towels, bed sheets, curtains. Commercial textiles: lace, trimmings, ropes, tarpaulins, sewing thread. Leisure textiles: awnings, art canvases. Blended and mixed, usually with cotton.

Linen fibre production (A-level only)

- The fibres are loosened from the flax plant stems using a process called retting.
- The retted stems are crushed in a process called scotching to separate the fibres from the woody outer bark.
- The fibres are heckled (combed) to remove the short fibres, leaving the long fibres.
- The processed linen fibres are spun into staple yarn.

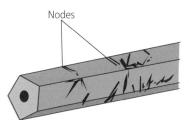

Figure 1.2.2 The structure of linen fibres

Ramie

Ramie is one of the oldest natural fibres. The high cost of fibre extraction and production reduces its competitiveness, however consumer demand for sustainable fibres is leading to increased use.

Ramie fibres can be harvested from the same plant up to three times a year, making it a highly sustainable fibre source.

> **Key terms**
>
> **Lustre:** a natural sheen that gives shine to a fibre.
>
> **Drape:** the way a fabric hangs or falls.

Table 1.2.3 Properties/characteristics of ramie and its uses

Properties/characteristics	Examples	Uses
Good absorbency, breathable. Keeps it shape and does not shrink. Harder to dye than cotton. Naturally white in colour. Has good strength. Poor elasticity, creases easily. Highly flammable. Poor insulator, cool to wear. Smooth lustrous appearance. Stiff and brittle handle. Resistant to mildew, light and insect attack. Biodegradable.	Ramie	Apparel fabrics: lightweight summer use. Home textiles: table linens, dish cloths. Commercial textiles: ribbon, sewing thread, sacks, twine and cord. Mostly blended with cotton, wool, polyester or acrylic.

Ramie fibre production (A-level only)

- The stems are harvested by cutting above the root.
- A laborious process of decortication (scraping and pounding) is used to remove the bark of the stem.
- The raw fibres are washed, dried and degummed using chemicals to extract the spinnable fibre.
- The processed ramie fibres are spun into staple yarn.

Figure 1.2.3 The ramie plant is native to eastern Asia

Natural animal/protein fibres

Wool

Wool comes from the fleece of a sheep. Wool fibres are classed according to their fineness, length, crimp and the breed of sheep they come from. They are staple fibres made from long chains of protein molecules.

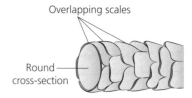

Figure 1.2.4 The structure of wool fibres

Table 1.2.4 Properties/characteristics of wool and its uses

Properties/characteristics	Examples	Uses
Water repellent and excellent moisture absorption. Anti-static as moisture is always present. Heat, moisture and mechanical action shrink and felt the fibres, making wool difficult to care for.	Worsted, baize, flannel, jersey, tweed, serge, fleece, tartan	Apparel fabrics: coats, suits, trousers, sweaters, hats, scarves, gloves, socks. Home textiles: blankets, carpets. Commercial textiles: loft insulation, noise insulation. Leisure textiles: horse rugs, athletic and leisure wear.
Adequate strength but not very durable. High natural fire resistance, self-extinguishes if set alight. Excellent elasticity, the natural crimp provides 'springiness', enabling creases to fall out. Good insulation/thermal qualities. No lustre because the fibres are not smooth. Origin, fineness and length of fibre determine the handle of wool fabrics. Wool can be soft or itchy. Biodegradable.		Blended and mixed usually with cotton, silk, polyester, acrylic and other animal hair fibres. Sportwool is a mix of merino wool and polyester fibres. The wool draws moisture away from the body, which is wicked away by the polyester, keeping the wearer cool.

Wool fibre production (A-level only)

- **Shearing:** the sheep's fleece is removed by hand typically once a year.
- **Sorting:** the longer fibres are separated from the shorter fibres. The longer fibres are processed through the worsted system to make high-end products such as suits. The shorter fibres are processed through the woollen system to make products such as blankets and sweaters.
- **Carbonising and scouring:** carbonising is a chemical process that removes vegetable matter such as seeds and grass. Scouring is a mechanical process that washes the fibres to remove the lanolin and dirt.
- **Carding:** disentangles clumps of fibres, aligns them parallel to one another in a web, which is then condensed into a continuous strand of fibres called a sliver. The sliver is processed further using a roving machine to compact and hold the fibres closer together, minimising the chance of breakage during spinning.
- **Spinning:** The rovings are fed into a mechanised spinning machine and a predetermined amount of twist is applied. The yarn is re-wound onto suitable packages for knitting or weaving.

Figure 1.2.5 The natural crimp in wool fibres

Animal hair (A-level only)

Luxurious animal fibres are expensive due to limited supply. They include:

- cashmere, from the undercoat of cashmere goats
- mohair, from angora goats
- angora, from angora rabbits.

Table 1.2.5 Properties/characteristics of animal hair and its uses

Properties/characteristics	Examples	Uses
Hair fibres have similar qualities to wool fibres: - naturally fire resistant - very good thermal insulators - soft, luxurious handle and appearance - biodegradable.	Cashmere fibres are very soft, lightweight, lustrous and three times more insulating than wool. Mohair fibres are long, lightly curled and have a silky lustre. They are naturally elastic, crease resistant and dye well. Angora fibres are very fine and lightweight. A hollow core makes the fibres very good at absorbing moisture vapour.	Apparel fabrics: luxury coats, suits, knitwear, shawls. Home textiles: luxury interior textiles. Can be used alone or blended with wool to reduce the cost.

Animal hair fibre production (A-level only)

- In the case of cashmere and angora, the fibres need to be washed and de-haired to remove the coarse guard hairs before being spun into yarn.
- Angora goats are shorn twice a year to collect the mohair fibres. The fibres are processed in a similar way to wool fibres but extra care is taken to try and keep the delicate fibres clean and free of debris.
- A wide range of animal hair fibres is used in the textile industry. Other examples include camel, alpaca, vicuna and horsehair.

Silk

Cultivated silk comes from the cocoon of the *Bombyx mori* silkworm. Vegans and animal rights activists consider cultivated silk production to be unethical as in commercial production, the moth is killed before it can emerge and damage the cocoon breaking the filament fibre.

Production of wild silk is on a smaller scale than cultivated silk. Wild silk comes from the cocoon of other species, for example the tussah silkworm. It is harvested after the moth has left the cocoon. The cocoons differ in colour and have a natural slub texture in the filament. Wild silks tend to be more difficult to unravel as the cocoon has been damaged.

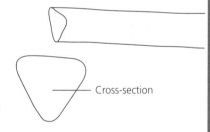

Figure 1.2.6 **The structure of silk fibres**

Table 1.2.6 Properties/characteristics of silk and its uses

Properties/characteristics	Examples	Uses
Excellent tensile strength due to the long continuous length of the fibre. Very absorbent. Anti-static as moisture is always present. Weak when wet, so is hard to care for. Extensible and elastic. Does not burn easily, self-extinguishes.	Bourette, chiffon, crêpe, crêpe de Chine, duchesse, habutai, organza, pongee, satin crêpe, taffeta, wild silk (tussah, Honan, shantung)	Apparel fabrics: formal wear, ties, blouses, lingerie, scarves. Home textiles: soft furnishings, bed sheets, wall hangings. Commercial textiles: surgical sutures, sewing and embroidery threads, ribbons. Blended as a staple fibre with wool.

Properties/characteristics	Examples	Uses
Cool and warm.		
Naturally lustrous.		
Pleasant handle and comfortable to wear.		
Has fluidity and drapes well.		
Weakened if exposed to sunlight and sweat.		
Biodegradable.		

Silk fibre production (A-level only)

● The silkworm produces the fibre when it pupates. Two filaments of silk fluid are extruded from spinnerets below the silkworm's mouth. Sericin (silk gum) coats the filaments and holds them together to produce a single filament fibre which, when wound around the body of the silkworm, creates a cocoon.

● To extract the fibre, cocoons are degummed by soaking them in boiling water. This kills the moths and softens the sericin.

● The long continuous fibre is unwound (reeled) from the cocoon and is spun with three to ten silk fibres to form a filament yarn.

Manufactured regenerated fibres

Manufactured regenerated fibres are made from natural cellulose that has been chemically modified (see Figure 1.2.7). Other examples of manufactured regenerated fibres include cupro, alginate and rubber.

> **Key term**
>
> **Solvent:** a chemical substance used to dissolve or dilute other substances or materials.

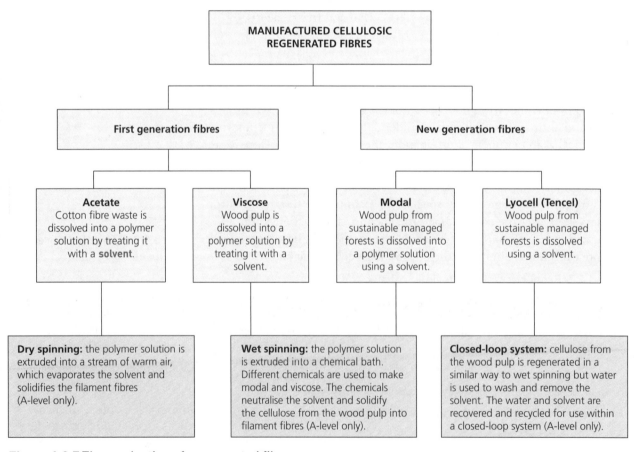

Figure 1.2.7 The production of regenerated fibres

Table 1.2.7 The common properties/characteristics of regenerated fibres and their uses

Properties/characteristics	Uses
Their structure allows similar or better levels of **absorbency** than cotton.	Fashion garments, lining fabric, lingerie, trims and ribbons.
The shape can be changed using **spinnerets** with different cross-sections (see Figure 1.2.11).	Can be used in their filament form or cut up and used as staple fibres.
They take dye and print techniques especially well.	Used in blends with natural fibres or on their own because of their reduced environmental impact.
Non-static as some moisture is always present.	
Easy care, but first generation fibres should not be tumble dried as they are prone to shrinking.	
Naturally breathable with good wicking properties.	
Low ability to trap air so cool to wear.	
First generation fibres have lower strength and resistance to abrasion than cotton.	
Same or slightly better resistance to creasing than cotton.	
Softer handle and better drape than cotton.	
The degree of lustre can be engineered from subtle to bright whereas cotton is a matt fibre.	
Similar flammability to cotton due to the cellulosic content.	
Lower resistance to damage from sunlight, bleach and microorganisms than cotton.	
Biodegradable and recyclable, and inexpensive to produce.	

Key terms

Absorbency: a fabric's ability to retain moisture; it affects a fabric's comfort, ease of care, dye-ability and static build-up.

Spinneret: the nozzle part of the spinning machine where the molten fibres are extruded.

First and second generation fibres

Developments in regenerated fibres have seen improvements in strength, softness and crease resistance.

Table 1.2.8 Distinguishing differences in individual regenerated fibres

First generation fibres	New generation fibres
Viscose: ● More absorbent than cotton and other regenerated fibres.	**Modal:** ● Stretched more than viscose after spinning to make fibres stronger. Can be tumble dried. ● Silky smooth, very soft handle and drape.

→

Figure 1.2.8 Striations on the longitudinal view of viscose fibres

First generation fibres	New generation fibres
Acetate: ● Lower absorbency, prone to static. ● More elastic than others but still creases. ● Thermoplastic capabilities. ● Subdued lustre and elegant drape.	**Lyocell (Tencel is a trade name for lyocell):** ● Stronger and more extensible than cotton so does not crease as much. ● Totally biodegradable, recyclable and made using a closed-loop system that reuses the chemicals used in the manufacturing process.

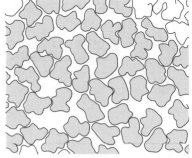

Figure 1.2.9 Irregular cross-section of viscose fibres

Synthetic fibres

General characteristics of synthetic fibres

● They are mostly manufactured using the melt spinning process, which produces very fine, smooth continuous filament fibres.
● The cross-section shape of a fibre can be engineered to give different properties and characteristics.
● The long, continuous filament fibres can be left in their original state, textured or cut up into staple form.
● They can be coloured during the manufacturing process (dope dyeing).
● Their **thermoplastic** properties enable them to be heat-set, and shaped and finished in a range of ways.
● The specific properties of each fibre are dependent on their chemical composition but most are very strong, non-absorbent, smooth and lightweight.
● They come from non-renewable sources and take many years to biodegrade.

> **Key term**
>
> **Thermoplastic:** a material that becomes soft and mouldable above a specific temperature and solidifies upon cooling.

Figure 1.2.10 Melt spinning of synthetic fibres

Figure 1.2.11 Spinneret shapes and man-made fibre cross-sections

Spinneret shapes and fibre cross-sections

Table 1.2.9 Properties/characteristics of different synthetic fibres and their uses

Name	Properties/characteristics	Uses
Polyamide (nylon) Produced as continuous smooth filaments including very fine microfibres.	Low absorbency, dries quickly, does not shrink, prone to static.	Clothing, tights, socks, underwear.
	Very strong and durable, high abrasion resistance.	Outdoor and active wear.

Name	Properties/characteristics	Uses
They can be textured or cut into staple fibres. Microfibre brand names include: ● Tactel Aquator, wicks moisture away from the body, used for underwear and sportswear fabric. ● Tactel Diablo, a lustrous fabric with good drape used for hosiery and lingerie.	Good elasticity and crease recovery. Low flammability, fabric melts and drips. Thermoplastic – fibres can be textured, desired creases can be heat-set or inadvertently added to fabric if washed at too high a temperature. Lightweight and can have lustre if the fibres are extruded as flat smooth surfaces that reflect a lot of light. Cross-section shape and fibre thickness can be engineered to provide fine, smooth, soft fabrics that drape well, or thicker, denser, stiffer fabrics. Fibre shape and texturing gives improved comfort and thermal qualities, enabling moisture to wick away from the body. Flat, smooth filaments trap little air so are cool and poor insulators. Weakens in sunlight and chlorine bleach but resistant to chemicals and microorganisms.	Tents, umbrellas. Carpets. In staple form, it is blended with most fibres.
Aramids (A-level only) Technical textiles developed from polyamide, brand names include: ● Kevlar ● Nomex.	Greater strength and durability. Stab and tear resistant. Fine and lightweight. Flexible for ease of movement. Nomex has similar properties to Kevlar and can withstand even higher temperatures.	Bullet- and stab-proof vests. Motor sport clothing. Industrial work wear.
Polyester Produced as continuous smooth filaments. They can be textured or cut into staple fibres. Microfibre trade name: Trevira Finesse.	Very similar properties to polyamide. The most commonly used synthetic fibre. Better thermoplasticity qualities than polyamide. Does not weaken in sunlight. Non-renewable source but can be recycled, e.g. Polartec fleece can be made from recycled drinks bottles.	A wider range of clothing, including outdoor and active wear. Bed sheeting. Lining fabric. Sewing thread. Wadding and fibre fill.
Acrylic Spun using the wet or dry spinning method. Mostly used as bulky staple fibres.	Low absorbency, prone to static. Easy care, dries quickly. Good strength. Sensitive to heat and highly flammable. Good elasticity, crease resistant. Good thermal qualities, soft and warm. Wool-like handle, with good drape. Poor lustre.	Knitting yarn. Knitwear. Fake fur. Carpet. Soft furnishing fabrics. Blended with wool or polyester.

➜

Name	Properties/characteristics	Uses
Chlorofibres (polyvinyl) (A-level only) Used in filament or staple form or as a coating.	Strong. Durable. Breathable, easy care, waterproof. Good insulator. PVC can be recycled.	Raincoats. Showerproof coatings. Thermal clothing. Active sportswear. Socks and underwear.
Fluorofibres (PTFE) (A-level only) Used mainly as a coating. Trade name: Teflon.	When applied to fabric as a finishing process, the fabric is: ● water repellent and stain resistant ● easy care and less energy is needed to dry the fabric ● durable and flexible ● breathable but windproof.	Used to protect fabrics, e.g. school trousers. Work wear. Soft furnishings. Shoes.
Elastomeric (elastane) Always used as the core in core-spun yarn and combined with natural and synthetic fibres. Brand name: Lycra.	Low absorbency and easy care. Good tear resistance and durability. Very fine and lightweight. Gives a high degree of comfort and allows free movement. Increases shape retention, crease recovery and improves drape in woven fabrics.	1–2% in socks or trousers. 15–20% as needed in swimwear, foundation wear or sportswear.

Inorganic fibres (A-level only)

Inorganic fibres are not synthetic polymers but are included in the man-made fibre classification.

Table 1.2.10 Classification of man-made inorganic fibres

Name	Processing method	Properties	Uses
Glass (fibreglass) Source: powdered mineral compounds.	A direct melt method is used to draw filament glass fibres from the molten mineral compound. The fibres can be used as filaments or cut into staple fibres.	High tensile strength but low extensibility. Poor abrasion resistance. High heat resistance and thermal conductivity. Impermeable and unaffected by sunlight, chemicals and microorganism attack. Non-stick, non-toxic and reflective.	Insulation material in buildings. Flame-retardant fabrics, e.g. theatre safety curtains. Strengthened glass, reinforced plastics. Hospital wall coverings.
Carbon (graphite fibre) Source: carbon created by burning acrylic fibre.	Carbon fibres are twisted together to form a yarn that can be used by itself or made into a fabric.	Very strong for its size. Lightweight. Abrasion and tear resistant. Flame resistant at very high temperatures. Resistant to chemicals.	Protective clothing. Intelligent electro-conductive fabrics for e-textiles. Aeroplane interiors, e.g. carpets, upholstery fabric. Production of nano-fibres.

Name	Processing method	Properties	Uses
Metal Source: copper, aluminium and steel for common uses. Titanium, gold and silver for special uses.	Very thin layers of metal are laminated between clear film and cut lengthwise into thin strips. Alternatively, the metal is heated until it vaporises and deposits at high pressure onto polyester fibres.	Strong and abrasion resistant. Lightweight. Withstands high temperatures. Good conductor of heat and electricity. Anti-bacterial and anti-microbial. Anti-static. Stiff handle and high lustre.	Decorative fabrics and trims, e.g. Lurex. Silver prevents a build-up of bacteria in sports clothing and medical applications. Conductive sewing thread in e-textiles.
Ceramic Source: powdered inorganic non-metallic materials such as crystalline oxide. Carbon and silicon are also considered ceramics.	Incorporated into synthetic fibres by coating them with ceramic particles or encapsulating them in the fibre.	Resistant to 1000°C+ temperatures. Lightweight and resistant to chemicals. Produces fabrics with UV protection. Has heat-deflection properties to regulate body temperature, e.g. Protective Ceramic Coating Material (PCCM). Has therapeutic properties if combined with body heat.	Industrial work wear. Swimwear, e.g. Esmo and Sunfit fabrics. A fabric's surface coated with PCCM deflects heat in hot weather. When applied to lining fabric, it deflects body heat back to the body. Bioceramic fabric, e.g. Under Armour Athlete Recover Sleep Wear. Production of nano-fibres. Thermolite, a lightweight fibre with a hollow core used in socks, sleeping bags and jackets.

> **Exam tip**
>
> Be able to explain how the cross-sectional and linear formations that occur in natural fibres and those engineered during synthetic and man-made fibre production can affect their performance and aesthetic characteristics.

Performance characteristics of yarns

REVISED

Fibres need to be made into yarns before they can be manufactured into woven and knitted fabrics.

Yarn can be made from staple fibres (staple yarns) or filament fibres (filament yarns). They can be manufactured with twist using a spinning process or, in the case of some multifilament or monofilament yarns, without twist using a winding process.

- Low-level twist produces a weaker, softer, bulkier yarn and makes it easier to form a raised **nap** if the fabric is finished using mechanical brushing.
- High-level twist produces a stronger, smoother and denser yarn.

> **Key term**
>
> **Nap:** a raised surface made by brushing the fabric surface after weaving.

- Too much twist causes the yarn to become crinkly. Crêpe fabric has a crinkled, crisp appearance and is made using highly twisted yarn.
- Plying a single yarn twisted in the S direction and a single yarn twisted in the Z direction makes a balanced yarn, which is less likely to untwist.

Tex and **denier** are technical terms relating to the formulae used to state a yarn's thickness.

Fibre type, thickness of yarn and the tightness of twist all affect a yarn's working and aesthetic properties. The choice of yarn is mostly dictated by the end use of a woven or knitted fabric.

Types of yarn

Staple yarns

- All manufactured fibres are produced as filaments but they are often cut into staple lengths to make staple yarn. This increases the range of yarn and fabric types.
- Staple yarns are hairy. They give fabrics texture and a soft, fuller handle. They are good insulators and mostly matt in appearance. Longer staple fibres give staple yarns a degree of lustre.
- Staple yarns are weaker than filament yarns as regularity in the thickness of the yarn is harder to achieve.
- They are more expensive to manufacture, as more stages and energy are required.
- Staple yarn can contain two or more different types of fibre. Staple fibres are blended to create aesthetic effects and improve performance and aftercare of fabrics. See page 28 for more detail on fibre blends.

Filament yarns

- Filament yarns are smoother and more regular than staple yarns, making them stronger.
- They give fabrics a more compact handle, a higher degree of lustre but are not so good at insulating.
- Silk filaments are very fine and need to be lightly twisted with other silk fibres so that they can be made into usable yarn.
- Man-made fibres are extruded from the spinneret as continuous filaments, which may be grouped together with or without twist to form a multifilament yarn.
- A monofilament yarn consists of one continuous filament spun from a spinneret with one hole.

Single yarns

A single or one-ply yarn is a continuous single thread of twisted staple or filament fibres, or a monofilament, or filaments grouped together without twist to make a single yarn.

Plied yarns

- Plied or folded yarns are made by twisting two or more single yarns together.
- Twisting the yarns together in the opposite direction to the way they were spun achieves uniform thickness and strength, and makes products like sewing thread fit for purpose.
- The use of single yarns made from different fibres or colours achieves special effects in plied and corded or cabled yarns.

> **Key terms**
>
> **Tex:** the metric system used to state the thickness of a yarn.
>
> **Denier:** a measure of thickness used for all filament yarns. The higher the denier number, the thicker the yarn.

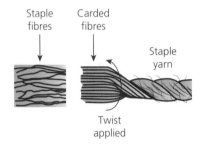

Figure 1.2.12 Staple yarn formation

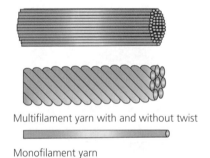

Multifilament yarn with and without twist

Monofilament yarn

Figure 1.2.13 Filament yarn formation

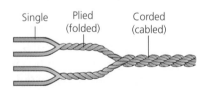

Figure 1.2.14 Multi-ply and corded yarns

Core-spun yarns

Core-spun yarns are multicomponent yarns. They have a filament core and a sheath made from staple or filament yarn. They are important in the manufacture of stretch and metallic yarns and sewing threads. See Chapter 1.3 (page 38) on threads.

The different methods of core-spinning fibres (A-level only)

● Core-spun yarn can be made by twisting a sheath of staple or filament yarn around a filament core made from a different fibre. Elastomeric fibre or a synthetic filament yarn is usually used as the core and synthetic or natural fibres as the sheath.

● Alternatively, to make a core yarn with elastane fibre, the elastane filament is stretched then covered with a sheath of non-elastic fibres. These may be natural or synthetic fibres, or a blend. The sheathed yarns are wrapped in opposite directions to balance the core-spun yarn.

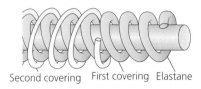
Second covering   First covering   Elastane

Figure 1.2.15 Core-spun yarn with elastomeric core

Textured yarns

● In their original smooth state, filament yarns have limited properties.

● Texturing processes add bulk and interest to yarns, making fabrics softer, more extensible, better insulators and able to retain or wick moisture away from the body.

● Most texturing methods depend on the thermoplastic nature of man-made fibres to heat-set permanent crinkles, creases or crimps along the length of the filaments.

● Textured yarn can be used in sportswear, swimwear, underwear and tights.

Sheath   Lycra core

Figure 1.2.16 The stretched elastane fibre is covered by a sheath of non-elastic fibres

Methods of texturing yarn (A-level only)

● False-twist texturing: smooth thermoplastic filament yarn is tightly twisted, heat-set and then untwisted.

● Air-jet texturing: this does not depend on thermoplastic properties so it can be used on any filament yarn. A jet of compressed air creates loops and tangles.

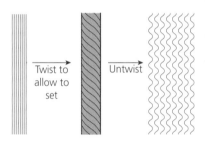
Twist to allow to set   Untwist

Figure 1.2.17 False twisting of thermoplastic yarns

Fancy yarns

● Fancy yarns change the appearance and handle of fabrics by adding irregularities and other effects. They are made using special spinning processes.

● They usually have a core, binder and effect yarn, each of which can be made out of any fibre and can be in staple or filament yarn form.

● Fancy yarns also provide multicolour effects by mixing fibres dyed different colours or by plying two or more different coloured yarns.

● Bouclé yarn: the looped yarn can add colour and give a textured bumpy feel to woven or knitted fabrics.

● Slub yarn: made by changing the spinning speed at irregular intervals to produce yarn with thicker and thinner sections. It gives an uneven texture similar to fabrics made from linen or wild silk.

● Chenille yarn: made by weaving and then cutting an open, net-type fabric into strips. Cut fibres jut out around the central core giving fabrics a fuzzy, bulky and soft appearance.

● Metallised yarn: gives an iridescent effect and is used to make fabrics such as lamé and brocades. Its method of manufacture is explained on page 39.

Bouclé yarn

Key
— Core yarn
= Binder yarn
∿ Effect yarn

Figure 1.2.18 Structure of bouclé yarn

Yarn mixtures and blends

Combining fibre properties in a yarn or a fabric makes a fabric with the specific qualities required for a particular end use.

- Blends are achieved by spinning two or more different fibres together to make a yarn.
- Staple yarns require the fibres to be the same length so they can be blended together before being spun into a yarn.
- Continuous filament yarns can be twisted together to make a multifilament yarn, for example polyester and polyamide.
- The different ratios of fibres to be blended are determined by the fibres used and the end product.
- In fabric, a mixture usually means the warp and weft yarns are made from different fibres.
- In a yarn, a mixture usually means it contains several elements, for example core-spun yarns made from elastomerics like Lycra and many other fibre types.

Table 1.2.11 The main reasons for blending yarns

Performance properties	To make a fabric stronger and more abrasion resistant.
	To make a fabric easier to care for and less prone to shrinking and creasing.
	To give improved comfort, absorbency, thermal insulation and stretch.
	To give thermoplastic properties to enable heat-setting.
Aesthetic appearance	To improve the texture and handle of a fabric.
	To give novelty effects when yarn or fabric is dyed since the uptake of dye by some fibres is better than others.
	To give improved colour or lustre.
Additional advantages	Blending reduces costs if a cheaper fibre is included.
	It allows for quicker washing and drying times, which are beneficial to the environment.
Disadvantages	Blends like polyester/cotton burn fiercely at high temperatures and give off toxic fumes. The cotton sets alight easily, it holds the polyester in place, which then melts and drips, causing severe burns.

Popular yarn blends include:

- polyester and cotton
- viscose and nylon
- wool and nylon
- polyester, wool and Lycra
- cotton and Lycra
- linen and polyester
- silk and polyester
- silk and cotton.

Performance characteristics of woven fabrics

REVISED

Woven fabrics are produced on a loom by interlacing yarns at right angles to one another:

- The warp yarns are fixed in the loom and run the length of the fabric.
- The weft yarns run across the fabric from selvedge to selvedge.

Types of weave

There are three main types of weave (plain, twill and satin) and all other weaves are variations on these types. Woven fabrics have relatively good strength and stability.

Table 1.2.12 The three main types of weave

Weave	Main characteristics	Example fabrics and uses
Plain (tabby) weave	Simplest and cheapest weave. Has the maximum number of interlacing points so makes a strong fabric. Fabric has a plain, firm surface, which makes it good for printing. Fabric looks the same on both sides. Dyed yarns in the weave can produce a variety of decorative effects. Fancy yarns introduce interest to the fabric, e.g. bouclé fabric. Highly twisted yarns create crêpe fabric.	Broderie anglaise, calico, canvas, chiffon, muslin, shirting, taffeta, voile, winceyette. A-level only: chambray, flannel, Madras, organdie, poplin. Typical uses: garment and interior products, sheeting.
Twill weave	The hardest-wearing weave. Fabric is more complex to make, so is more expensive than a plain weave. The interlacing of the weft and warp is offset to give a diagonal pattern. More variations are possible, depending on how many warp yarns the weft passes over. Fabric is firm, but frays due to fewer interlacing points. Fabric has a definite right and wrong side. The uneven surface pattern shows less dirt than other fabrics.	Cavalry twill, denim, drill, gabardine, tartan. A-level only: dog-tooth check, herringbone tweeds, serge. Typical uses: tailored outfits or work wear.
Satin weave	The warp yarn 'floats' over four or more weft yarns before going under one. Fabric has a right and wrong side as the weft yarns are almost completely hidden by the warp yarns. Fabric is not hard-wearing, it frays and snags easily due to fewer interlacing points. The use of filament yarns and longer 'floats' give fabrics a greater lustre. Not many variations are possible.	Satin, sateen, lighter-weight satins for linings and lingerie. A-level only: duchesse satin and heavy bridal satins. Typical uses: lingerie, bridal wear.

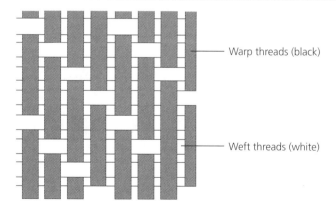

Figure 1.2.19 A 3/1 twill weave

Warp threads (black)

Weft threads (white)

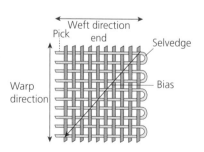

Figure 1.2.20 Plain weave

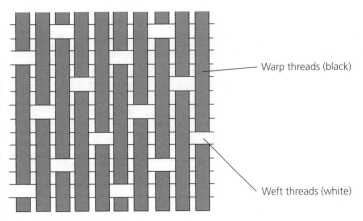

Warp threads (black)

Weft threads (white)

Figure 1.2.21 Satin weave

Key terms

Jacquard fabrics: fabrics where the pattern is created through weaving or knitting rather than being printed onto the fabric.

Pile weaves: classified as three-yarn system weaves as a third yarn is woven in with the warp and weft to make a fabric with a raised surface.

Table 1.2.13 Variations in weaves

Weave	Main characteristics	Example fabrics and uses
Jacquard weave (or knitting)	A computer-controlled jacquard loom lifts individual warp yarns and interchanges plain, twill and satin weaves to create complex patterns. Brocade is a stiff, heavy fabric; it has a definite right side and is expensive. It has an embroidered appearance and can include metallic yarns. Damask has a reversible embossed appearance.	Brocade is used in formal wear or in expensive furnishing fabrics. Damask is used in furnishing fabrics.
Warp **pile weave**	Two fabrics are woven face-to-face, a knife moves back and forth to cut the third (pile) yarn and separate the two fabrics. Warp pile fabrics are difficult to work with. Fabric is expensive due to the third yarn and fabric wastage from having to use a with nap layplan. Fabric is not durable as the third yarn can easily fall away from the background weave, leaving bald patches. A heavy, warm, soft plush fabric is created with good drape but is usually dry clean only.	Velvet is used in garments, upholstery and soft furnishing fabrics.
Weft pile weave	The cut weft loops produced during weaving create a ribbed pile (cords) that runs parallel to the selvedge. The cords vary in width, jumbo cord is very wide, needlecord is very fine. As with velvet, the fabric is expensive to produce and has similar working characteristics and challenges. Weft pile fabrics can be machine washed inside out with fastening such as zips closed.	Corduroy and needlecord are used in garments, upholstery and soft furnishing fabrics.
Uncut loop pile weave	The loops are uncut making a much stronger and more durable pile weave fabric. Fabric is expensive due to the amount of yarn used. Fabric is usually made with cotton fibres so it is soft, very absorbent and thermally insulating due to the extra yarn and the loop structure. Fabric takes a long time to dry and is very heavy when wet. Fabric frays and ravels when cut, and its weight and thickness can make it challenging to work with.	Terry towelling used in towels and bathrobes.

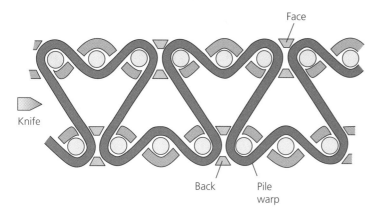

Figure 1.2.22 Velvet manufacturing

Figure 1.2.23 Brocade fabric

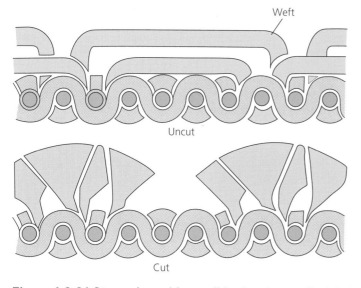

Figure 1.2.24 Stages in making a ribbed weft cut pile fabric

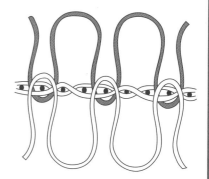

Figure 1.2.25 A terry weave showing the loops above and below the weave

Special woven effects (A-level only)

Pattern can be introduced into woven fabric using different coloured warp and weft yarns.

- **Stripes:** two or more different blocks of colours in the warp and one colour in the weft creates stripes.
- **Checks:** blocks of different coloured dyed yarn in both the warp and the weft creates checks.
- **Gingham:** equal blocks of two different coloured yarns in both the warp and the weft give an even-sized check.
- **Tartan:** alternating different-sized bands of coloured yarn (traditionally wool) are interlaced in the warps and wefts using a plain or twill weave to create the large check pattern.
- **Madras:** commercial production is similar to tartan but brightly coloured dyed cotton yarn and a plain weave is used to create a large check pattern.

Fabric effects created using fibres and yarns (A-level only)

- **Bouclé fabric:** bouclé yarn creates a bulky, plain-woven fabric that can have different colours and a textured hairy, knotty surface. Bouclé fabric is made from wool or acrylic or a wool/acrylic blend.

- **Crêpe fabric:** highly twisted unbalanced yarns create a soft fabric that drapes well and has an irregular crinkled appearance. A plain or special crêpe weave is used with silk, wool or polyester fibres and variations include crêpe de Chine and satin-backed crêpe.
- **Crinkles and permanent creasing:**
  - On cotton fabric, these can be achieved by printing a striped pattern using a caustic soda solution, which causes the treated area to shrink and crinkle. Or, alternative blocks of tight and loose warps can be used in the loom, so that the stripes are crinkled and flat. This fabric is called seersucker.
  - If thermoplastic fibres are present in the fabric, planned or random pleats or creases can be permanently heat-set into the fabric.
- **Crease- and shrink-resistant fabric:** using thermoplastic fibres in the fabric make it crease- and shrink-resistant. Post-weaving processes can distort a fabric; a stenter machine pulls the fabric into its intended size and shape, and heat-setting permanently holds it in place. The fabric will not shrink and will only crease if the fabric is washed at too high a temperature by the end user.
- **Metallic effects:** see special effects threads in Chapter 1.3, page 39.
- **Multi-coloured fabrics:** the uptake of dyes by some fibres is better than others, so using different fibres in a fabric or different dyes makes it possible to get interesting colour effects.

Performance characteristics of knitted fabrics

REVISED

Knitted fabrics are made of interlocking loops using one or more yarn. The two main types of looping are weft knit and warp knit. All other knitted fabrics are variations of these types. Knitted fabrics have fluidity, elasticity and stretch.

Types of knit

Table 1.2.14 Weft knit and warp knit

Knit	Main characteristics	Example fabrics and uses
Weft knit A single yarn travels the width of the fabric, in the same way that a weft yarn does in a woven fabric. Each successive row of loops links with the previous row of loops in the fabric.	Simplest knit. Can be produced by hand or by machine. Very stretchy and distorts easily when washed. Drapes softly and is figure-hugging. Does not crease easily. Fabric traps air and is a good insulator in still air. Moving air is able to get through the gaps in the fabric, making it cool to wear in these conditions. It snags, ladders and unravels easily. Has a definite right and wrong side. Is used to create tubular fabrics for seamless garments.	Single jerseys (plain knit). Double jerseys (look the same on both sides). Rib knits (used for cuffs and sweater hems). Sliver knits (pile-type fabric). Jacquard knits (complex patterns with coloured yarns). Polartec fleece (brushed weft-knitted fabric with an extra yarn knitted in to trap air and give a soft dense nap). Typical uses: wide range of garments and socks.

Warp knit		
Individual yarns are interlocked sideways along the length of the fabric in the same way that the warp yarn runs parallel to the selvedge of a woven fabric. Each needle loops its own yarn.	More complex structure. Can only be produced by machine. Less stretchy, gives a firmer fabric Does not ladder or unravel so can be cut and sewn more easily. Faster than weft knitting. Cheapest and fastest method of fabric production using yarns. A wider variety of knits can be produced.	Tricots (used in lingerie). Locknit fabrics (used in swimwear, hosiery and garments). Knitted velour (similar handle and appearance to velvet but stretchy). Raschel knits (resemble crocheted, lace, net or mesh fabrics). Knitted lace fabrics (used in garments and curtains). Typical uses: geotextiles and biotextiles.

Hand- and machine-knitted methods (A-level only)

- **Hand knitting:** has a craft aesthetic and is used to make individual products. Traditional styles of hand knitting include Aran (cable and lattice patterns), Fair Isle (multi-coloured patterns) and Guernsey (cable knit).
- **Machine knitting:** can be done on flat or circular industrial knitting machines. Flatbed machines have a row of needles that produce a wide width of fabric. Circular machines make a tube of knitting.
- **Panel knitting (pieces with integral welts):** individual, flat, rectangular panels including a finished-off edge for the cuff or waistband, are knitted. The garment parts are then cut to shape and assembled.
- **Fully fashioned panels:** the garment parts are knitted to the required shape and size and then stitched together to make the garment. This process is used to manufacture high-quality garments and hand-knitted garments.
- **Whole garment knitting:** knits a garment three-dimensionally in one piece. It is more sustainable as there is no waste and the seam-free garments don't break a garment's flow, making them comfortable to wear and easier to move in. They are used in sports, medical and wearable smart technology.

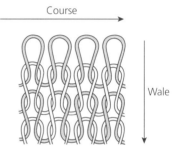

Figure 1.2.26 Basic weft knit

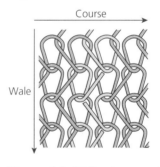

Figure 1.2.27 Basic warp knit

Performance characteristics of non-woven fabrics

REVISED

Non-woven fabrics are produced directly from fibres. They include felts and bonded fabrics. The process used depends on fibre type and the end-use requirements.

- The absence of yarn means felted fabrics lack strength and are difficult to maintain.
- Non-woven fabrics can be made in a range of weights, they are stiff, have no stretch and do not drape well.
- They do not fray, and cut easily with scissors or a laser.
- They are cheap to produce, making them suitable for disposable or one-use products.
- They have no grain, so a layplan is not needed, making them economical in use.
- The fibre webs are good thermal insulators, they also absorb sound and can be made flame retardant.

> **Key term**
>
> **Non-woven fabric:** made directly from fibres.

- Non-woven fabrics can be moulded into shapes.
- Some non-woven fabrics can be recycled and some can be made from recycled fibres.

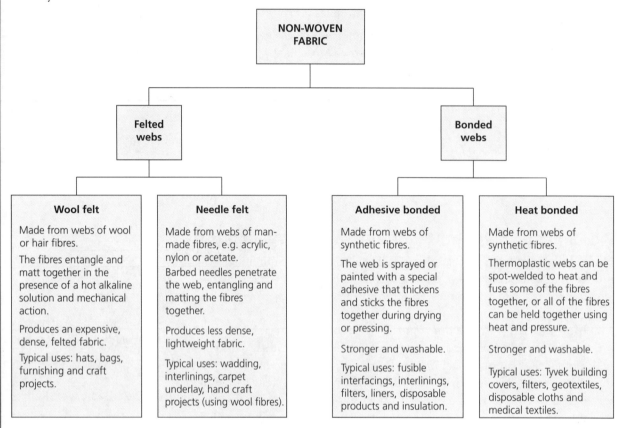

Figure 1.2.28 Production methods of non-woven fabrics

Smart materials

Smart materials are able to react to external stimuli or changes in their environment without human intervention. They revert to their original state once the stimuli have been removed.

External stimuli include changes in temperature, light levels and pressure (force).

Smart materials include ones that:
- monitor body functions and administer medicines or give warnings, for example Mamagoose baby monitoring pyjamas
- maintain a personal microclimate, for example Stomatex, Outlast
- have chromatic properties and change colour in response to specific situations, for example heat sensitive bandages that indicate infection
- have shape memory, for example Corpo Nove shirts, which adjust to differing temperatures
- are self-cleaning, for example nano-technology fabrics triggered by sunlight
- can generate solar power when exposed to sunlight.

> **Key term**
>
> **Smart material:** a material that is able to react to external stimuli or changes in its environment without human intervention.

> **Typical mistake**
>
> Don't confuse smart materials with technical/modern materials. Know the specific names and uses for smart materials. In your answers, include the stimuli that cause smart materials to change and the way in which they change, for example a colour change due to a change in temperature.

Technical textiles

Technical textiles are manufactured for non-aesthetic purposes where function is the primary criterion. They are new materials that have been developed from their original form.

Technical and **modern materials** include the following examples:
- Gore-Tex
- Kevlar and Nomex
- Phosphorescent textiles, for example high-visibility safety clothing and novelty clothing. Textiles finished with phosphorescent dyes glow in the dark. The pigment is able to absorb light energy, store it and later emit it.
- Reflective textiles using glass beads, for example 3M Scotchlite reflective material.
- **Microencapsulated fibres**, for example those that release scents or beneficial chemicals by sensory perception technology, such as moisturising tights. The chemicals are incorporated into the core of core-spun microfibre yarn.
- Microfibres, for example Tactel Aquator, Tactel Diablo and Trevira Finesse.

Materials using nano-technology (A-level only)

Ceramic and carbon fibres are important in the production of **nano-fibres** because they are extremely lightweight and very strong. The tiny fibres are made using an electro-spinning process, and are collected in the form of sheets that resemble non-woven felt. These sheets of fabric can be used as breathable membranes. Carbon fibres are used in the production of electro-conductive fibres, which are used to make intelligent fabrics or wearable computers.

Performance characteristics of fabrics

The interrelationship between the following factors determines the overall performance characteristics of a fabric:
- the fibre, or blend or mixture of fibres used
- the yarn structure (not applicable in non-woven fabrics)
- the way the fibres or yarns are incorporated to construct the fabric
- the way the fabric is finished.

The end use determines what performance characteristics are required in a fabric. Fundamental performance characteristics include: strength, durability, elasticity, flammability, thermal qualities, absorption, water resistance, **formability**, handle, drape, **weight** and **rip-proofing**.

Colour, **repeat pattern**, **directional pile**, nap, texture and lustre are additional features that can influence the sales potential of a fabric.

Now test yourself

1. Using examples, explain the difference between smart textiles and technical/modern textiles. Include definitions in your answer.
2. Explain why Kevlar fibres are suitable for use in a stab-proof vest worn by the emergency services.
3. Using examples, explain the key differences between first and new generation manufactured regenerated fibres.
4. Explain the difference between a fibre blend and a fabric mixture, and give three reasons why fibres are blended to make fabric.
5. How do bonded, non-woven fabrics differ from felted, non-woven fabrics?

Key terms

Technical/modern materials: new materials that have been developed from their original form.

Microencapsulated fibre: a microfibre that has tiny capsules containing health or cosmetic chemicals embedded into its hollow centre.

Nano-fibre: an extremely lightweight strong fibre that is less than one micron in diameter.

Key terms

Formability: the ability to manipulate and shape fabrics without damaging them.

Weight: the outcome of how a fabric has been woven, its finish and sometimes the fibre type.

Rip-proof/rip-stop fabric: has a distinctive woven-in raised square pattern that stops the fabric from ripping or tearing.

Repeat pattern: the distance between one point of a design and the exact point where it begins again.

Directional pile: the raised surface on a fabric that appears to change colour when viewed from different angles.

Part 1 Technical principles

1.3 Methods of joining and use of components

Seams

Seams join pieces of fabric together. A good seam will be:

- strong and durable
- smooth and even, and protected from fraying
- accurately sewn so that the pattern pieces fit together and the finished product is the planned size.

Table 1.3.1 Types of seams and their uses

Seam type	Characteristics	Uses
Plain/open seam Pins, Tacking, Seam line, Wrong side, Reverse matching to finish ends, Wrong side **Figure 1.3.1 Making a plain seam**	Needs edge finishing to stop fraying during wear and washing. Simple and quick to construct. The most commonly used seam. Strong but not suitable for products that undergo a lot of strain. Gives a flat surface. Not visible on right side of opaque fabric. Used to create curved seams. Piping or cording can be inserted to give a decorative effect.	Suitable for all normal-weight fabrics. Used in most garments, household textiles and sporting goods.
French seam Stitch plain seam 10mm from edge. Trim seam allowance to 3mm. Turn to right side. Press flat. Stitch exactly on the seam line 5mm away. Right side, Fabric wrong sides together, Wrong side **Figure 1.3.2 Making a French seam**	**Self-finishing** as all raw edges are enclosed. More challenging and time consuming to construct. Strong as the seam is stitched twice. Not seen on the outside of a product but can be bulky. Aftercare is determined by product type and fabric used.	Used with delicate, fine, sheer fabrics that are prone to fraying such as chiffon and organza. Suitable for lightweight clothing, lingerie and children's wear.
Fell/double machined seam Press 5mm under, Place fabric wrong sides together and stitch on seamline, Fold over seamline, Press seam open. Trim one seam allowance to 5mm, Stitch folded edge over **Figure 1.3.3 Making a fell seam**	Self-finishing as all raw edges are enclosed. Challenging and time consuming to construct. Very strong and durable as the seam is stitched twice. Gives a decorative feature, the parallel lines of stitches can be seen and are often sewn in a contrasting coloured thread.	Used on products that have to withstand heavy wear and frequent washing such as shirts, jeans, trousers, overalls and other hardwearing garments.

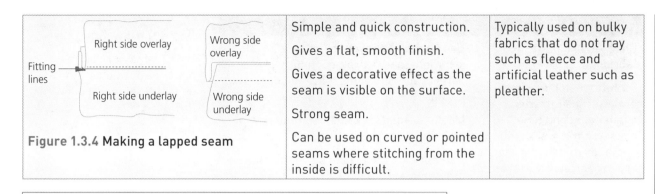

		Simple and quick construction.	Typically used on bulky fabrics that do not fray such as fleece and artificial leather such as pleather.
		Gives a flat, smooth finish.	
		Gives a decorative effect as the seam is visible on the surface.	
		Strong seam.	
		Can be used on curved or pointed seams where stitching from the inside is difficult.	

Figure 1.3.4 Making a lapped seam

> **Key term**
>
> **Self-finishing seam:** raw edges of the seam are enclosed within the seam as it is constructed.

Edge finished seams

Plain seams need to have an edge finish as they are not self-finished like other seams. Edge finishes give a neat appearance and prevent fraying, helping to increase the life of a product.

The edge finishing method chosen will depend on the fabric used and the position of the seam on the product. Edge finishing techniques include: edge stitching, overlocking, pinking and binding.

Techniques for working with different fabric types

Techniques for working with different fabric types are shown in Table 1.3.2.

Table 1.3.2 Techniques for working with different fabric types

Fabric type	Working techniques
Knitted fabric	Avoid stretching the fabric when pinning and cutting out.
	Finish seam edges using an overlocker.
	Use a stretch stitch with polyester thread as it is strong and has some give.
	Use a ballpoint needle to prevent **snagging**.
	Stich in stay tape to stabilise seams where stretch is not needed.
	Use interfacing to strengthen and stop components from sagging.
	Press seams open using a roller.
Stretch fabrics	Use a stretch stitch with polyester sewing thread to enable seams and hems to stretch with the fabric.
	Use a fine ballpoint needle to prevent snagging.
	Use stretch interfacing to maintain stretch but increase stability.
	Press stretch fabrics under a dry cloth using a warm iron.

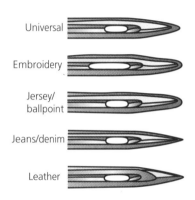

Figure 1.3.5 Sewing machine needles

> **Key term**
>
> **Snagging:** a defect in a textile product caused by pulling or plucking yarns from a fabric surface.

Fabric type	Working techniques
Checked and patterned fabrics Pattern-matching check or patterned fabric is challenging and time consuming to work with. Perfectly matched products are expensive, as a lot of fabric is wasted.	Use a **with nap layout** to achieve symmetry and overall continuity of the pattern across seams, pockets, darts and facings. Match, pin and tack seams at the sewing line and not at the cutting line. Cut fabric on the bias to solve matching problems. Use a walking foot to stop seams moving when machine stitched.
Directional fabrics These fabrics have a one-way pattern design or **nap**.	Use a with nap layout to avoid pattern and shade variations in the finished product. Pin in the seam allowance to prevent directional fabrics being marked. Use fine, sharp needles to prevent snagging. Finish seam edges as early as possible to prevent fraying. Use a walking foot to stop seams moving when machine stitched. Use a needleboard to protect a fabric's pile when pressing. Iron directional fabrics only on the wrong side (WS).
Sheer fabrics Include chiffon and organza. Because the inner structure of garments is visible, careful sewing and pressing are essential.	Sandwich the fabric in tissue paper to prevent sliding or mangling when sewn. Work with fine pins, sharp needles and scissors to avoid snagging. Pin in the seam allowance and use narrow self-finishing French seams. Keep the fabric (and tissue paper) taut when sewing, to prevent puckering. Use the same fabric to strengthen areas where components or trims are sewn. Press seams over a thick towel to stop a ridge showing on the right side (RS).

Key terms

With nap layout: all the paper pattern pieces must lie in the same direction on the fabric.

Directional fabric: fabric that has a definite one-way pattern or nap.

Nap: a raised surface made by brushing the fabric surface after weaving. On pile fabrics, such as velvet, the fabric will feel different when brushed in opposite directions and will appear to change colour when viewed from different angles. Satin woven fabric is lustrous and the nap will be noticeable if the pieces are cut going in the wrong direction.

Threads

REVISED

Machine and sewing threads

- **Polyester fibres** are mostly used to make general-purpose sewing threads because:
  - they are strong
  - they have a degree of give so are good to use with stretch fabrics and fabrics containing synthetic fibres
  - they do not shrink
  - they are resistant to rot.
- Polyester fibres in their filament form are not used on their own as the friction created by a machine needle when sewing causes them to soften

and break. The filaments are either covered with a sheath of cotton fibres (core spun) or cut to staple length and spun into sewing thread.

- For ease of care, it is preferable for the sewing thread to have the same fibre composition as the fabric being used.
- **Specialist threads:** buttonhole thread is a thicker thread made from polyester or silk, and is used for hand-stitched buttonholes, sewing on buttons and topstitching. Other specialist threads include overlocking thread, elastic thread, invisible thread, fusible thread and quilting thread.

Embroidery threads

- **Stranded embroidery cotton thread:** the cotton fibres are mercerised to improve dye uptake, strength and lustre, and reduce shrinkage. It has six easily separable strands that enable variation in the weight of stitches.
- **Machine embroidery thread:** usually made from viscose fibres. Popular brands include Madeira and Gütermann. Viscose has good tensile strength, a high lustre and a soft, flexible handle. It runs smoothly at high speed, with low incidences of thread breakage.

Special effect threads

- **Metallic threads:** can be core-spun by loosely wrapping fine yarn around very fine strips of metal laminated between clear synthetic film. Or by wrapping coloured metallic foil around a polyester, viscose or nylon core thread.
- **Metallic-effect threads:** appear to be made out of metal but synthetic fibres are used to give a highly lustrous 3D effect. They are easier to work with.
- **Glow-in-the-dark threads:** made from coated polyester impregnated with a phosphorescent pigment. The thread is 'charged' by exposure to bright light and will glow in the dark.
- **Multi-coloured or variegated threads:** have a repeating multi-coloured dye pattern running throughout.

> **Key term**
>
> **Rouleau loop:** a thin tube of sewn and turned bias-cut fabric used to fasten dome-shaped buttons or frog fastenings.

Fusible fleece

REVISED

Bondaweb is a commercially available fusible fleece fabric. It is a soft, double-sided adhesive web that is attached to transfer paper. The heat of an iron melts the adhesive. It is used to temporarily bond one fabric to another.

Use of fastenings

REVISED

A wide variety of fastenings can be used depending on the effects to be achieved, the fabric type and end use of the product.

Table 1.3.3 Types of fastenings and their characteristics and uses

Type of fastening	Characteristics and uses
Buttons and buttonholes and loops	Most buttons are flat and are sewn onto fabric by hand or machine through two or four holes.
	Some buttons are dome shaped and have shanks (stems) through which they are sewn onto fabric.
	Buttons can be fastened using buttonholes or decorative **Rouleau loops**.
	Buttonholes must be sewn on a double layer of fabric that has been strengthened with interfacing.

Type of fastening	Characteristics and uses
Zips	Zips with metal or moulded plastic teeth are ideal for medium to heavyweight garments, sporting and outdoor applications.
	Zips with a polyester coil are lightweight and commonly used in fine-fabric fashion garments.
	Zips are secure fastenings but if they break they are hard to repair and the product may become unusable and be discarded.
Poppers and press-studs	Poppers or snap fasteners are used to fasten an opening where a smooth flat closure is desired.
	They are inserted using special tools. If a popper breaks or is not accurately lined up, it is impossible to replace as a hole is left in the fabric where the original popper was placed.
	Press-studs do the same job but are not decorative or as economical, as they need sewing on by hand.
Clips	A clip is a two-piece, quick-release fastening. Clips are commonly made from durable plastic and are sewn onto the end of webbing straps, which are stitched onto the product. An example is a parachute clip.
	They are used on luggage and sporting equipment applications.
Buckles	Buckles are used to fasten narrow products such as belts or bag straps.
	They have an open rim with a centre bar, with or without prongs.
	Buckles without prongs and eyelet holes are called buckle slides. These buckles are not secure fastenings as the two sides can slip out of alignment.
Clasps	A clasp is a two-part fastener where one side fastens into the other.
	Clasps are made out of metal or plastic and are used in a range of products including bags, coats and swimwear.
Velcro	Velcro consists of two fabric tapes. One tape has tiny nylon hooks and the other a soft, furry, looped surface. When the tapes are pressed together the hooks grip the loops to form a secure closure.
	The tapes can be cut to any length or shape. They are durable, virtually unbreakable, easy care and come in many colours, widths and weights.
D-rings	D-rings come in various sizes and are made from metal or plastic.
	They are used to alter the length of bag straps and belts.
	They are not very secure fastenings as they rely on friction between the strap and rings to stay in place.
Hooks and eyes	Hooks and eyes are a discreet, two-part fastening made from metal.
	They are used to fasten: • foundation garments such as bras • where edges meet at the top of a garment, e.g. on a dress • where edges overlap on waistbands, e.g. on trousers.
	They are used in a position of strain, as a degree of strain is necessary for the hook to remain fastened in the eye or bar.
Fabric and ribbon ties	Ties are decorative fastenings made from a range of materials including ribbon and bias binding.
	They are not very secure but are cheap and easy to use.
	If used on children's clothing/toys, they must comply with strict BSI safety regulations to avoid strangulation.

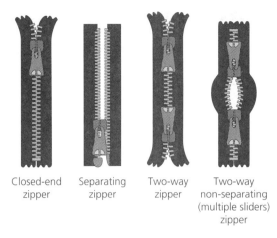

Closed-end   Separating   Two-way   Two-way
zipper   zipper   zipper   non-separating
                                 (multiple sliders)
                                 zipper

Figure 1.3.6 Zipper variations

Trims

Trims are mostly decorative components that add interest and finishing touches to products. They are chosen carefully to complement a product's fabric, style, use and aftercare.

Table 1.3.4 Types of trims and their characteristics and uses

Trim	Characteristics	Uses
Braids	Braids are usually long and narrow. Cords are circular braided materials. Complex structures or patterns are formed by plaiting or weaving braids.	Decorative edge trims sewn onto garments or craft projects. Formal garments and dress uniforms.
Ribbon	Woven with fine warp yarns with a high warp density. The long edges are finished but the cut short edge frays. Made from polyester and silk to give a lustrous appearance.	Used as tie fastenings or as a decorative trim on the edges of clothing or furnishings.
Piping	Piping consists of a strip of bias-cut fabric that is folded over a cord and inserted and sewn into a seam. Piping cord is made from cotton or polyester fibres. Fine cord is used for garments and thicker cord is used for soft furnishings.	Used to define style lines in garments. Strengthens areas vulnerable to abrasion in soft furnishings.
Edging	Edgings such as scalloped lace trims, braids and fringing come with finished edges.	Decorative edge trims sewn onto finished products.
Bindings	Strips of fabric that have been diagonally cut across the cross or bias grain of the fabric and sewn together makes bias binding. Bias binding can stretch and follow curves without creasing.	Used to edge textile products or cover the raw edge turnings of plain seams.
Fringing	Fringing can be: ● a decorative border of twisted warp threads left loose from a raveled edge of woven fabric ● looped threads, cords, beads or tassels attached to a separate braid or fabric trim ● narrow strips of material, which are held together at the top.	Used as edgings for: interior products such as cushions and curtains. Used as ornamental trim on flags and uniforms, fashion garments, dance and period costumes.

→

Trim	Characteristics	Uses
Lace	Lace is usually made from cotton, polyester, rayon or silk. It can be sewn onto edges to hide hems or appliqued onto surfaces to accentuate areas of the body such as necklines. It has delicate, weblike patterns that snag easily and need careful aftercare.	Used on special occasion wear, wedding dresses, lingerie, table linen and trimming on children's socks.
Beads	Beads add lustre and texture. In trim form they can be machined or hand sewn onto fabrics. Strong fabrics or interfaced weaker fabrics are needed to support the weight of the beads. Fabrics trimmed with beads are usually dry clean only.	Used to emphasise style lines in garments. Used to create patterns on products.
Diamanté	Diamanté or rhinestone gems mimic diamonds. They need to be glued onto fabric or they come with a pre-glued base that is activated by heat. Detergents damage the glue so careful laundering is needed.	Used on special occasion wear, belts, shoes and children's clothing.

Components and their appropriateness for a range of products

REVISED

Textile components are pre-manufactured items (bought ready made) that help finish a textile product. They include thread, fastenings, trims and e-components. Components should be chosen with care, as they need to be:
- suitable for the style and function of the textile product
- compatible with the fibre content, structure, weight and aftercare of the fabric used
- safe and efficient when meeting the needs of the end user
- within budget and readily obtainable
- suitable for use with existing manufacturing equipment and machinery.

E-components

Electronic components such as lights and tracking devices are integrated into textile products to add decorative and functional features. To work, the e-components must be part of a circuit and have a power source. Conductive sewing thread is used to connect the e-components to a low-voltage power source such as coin cell battery.

Examples of e-components include:
- wearable sensors that monitor temperature, moisture and medical devices
- integrated communication systems
- sound effects.

Figure 1.3.7 Wearable electronics

Interfacings, underlinings, linings and interlinings

REVISED

Extra layers of fabric are found in most garments as they can make an important difference to the finished product.

Table 1.3.5 Interfacings, underlinings, linings and interlinings

Type of product	Characteristics	Uses
Interfacings	Interfacing (shown in red) is an extra layer of fabric used under or between the outer layer(s) of fabric. It comes in different weights and colours, and is sew-in or iron-on. It is important to choose an interfacing closest to the properties of the outer fabric. It is applied before garment construction begins.	Interfacing helps to: ● give a crisp shape ● strengthen fabric to support fastenings ● stop fabric from stretching ● stabilise fabric for embroidery.
Underlinings	Underlining (shown in orange) is cut to the same shape and size as the outer fabric. It is sewn to the wrong side of the outer fabric and is then treated as one layer as the garment is made. The fabric should be lightweight and have the same aftercare requirements as the outer fabric. Possible fabrics are cotton muslin, satin and organza. Underlined garments can also be lined.	Underlining helps to: ● maintain the shape of a garment without stiffening it ● support seams in loose-weave fabrics ● provide opacity to sheer and lace fabrics, making them less see-through.
Linings	Lining (shown in blue) is constructed separately and attached to the product at facing or hem areas. Garments can be fully or partially lined. Lining fabrics are usually made from polyester, acetate or silk, and can be woven or knitted. The lining fabric should ideally have the same care requirements as the main fabric. An anti-static finish can be applied to stop static cling.	Lining helps to: ● make a product's insides look attractive and gives options for pockets ● cover and protect the garment's internal construction ● make garments warmer, more comfortable, and easier to put on and take off ● maintain the garment's shape so it hangs well ● protect the outer fabric from perfume and sweat.
Interlinings	Interlining (shown in green) is a fabric layer added to a garment. The interlining fabric should be soft and lightweight. Suitable fabrics include polyester wadding or fleece and brushed cotton fabric. The easiest way to add interlining is to sew it as one with the lining. Interlined garments can also be underlined and have interfaced sections.	Interlining helps to: ● make garments warmer or products like curtains better insulators ● add body to a garment to improve its drape.

Typical mistake

Confusion sometimes occurs between interfacings, underlinings, linings and interlinings. Make sure you know the difference between each type of fabric, and be able to explain where, why and how each fabric is used in textile products.

Exam tip

Practise writing step-by-step instructions that explain the correct order of processes needed to apply a range of components to a range of textile products. Use labelled diagrams to help with descriptions of the processes.

1.4 The use of finishes

Fabric finishes
REVISED

Fabric finishes modify a fabric to improve it or give it properties it does not naturally possess.

The most efficient and usual stage to add a finish is to apply it directly to the fabric before a product is manufactured. Alternatively, a finish can be applied at the garment stage, for example permanent creases can be heat-set into synthetic uniform trousers to improve ease of care and aesthetic appearance.

Table 1.4.1 Advantages and disadvantages of finishes

Advantages	Disadvantages
• Most fibres have disadvantages that can be cancelled out by applying fabric finishes. • Finishes enable specific products to conform to British Standards, e.g. children's nightwear. • They improve the function, performance and aesthetics of a product. • They give 'added value'. • They can extend a product's lifespan. • They improve easy-care performance, which is beneficial for both the consumer and the environment.	• Finishes are an additional processes and cost money. • Some fabrics need several finishes to make them suitable for their intended use. • Some finishes have negative effects on fabrics. • Some finishes are semi-permanent. • The chemicals used in finishes and their application can have a negative effect on the environment and the health and well-being of factory workers.

Mechanical finishes
REVISED

Mechanical finishes modify a fabric's surface using dry processes. They are applied using machinery.

Table 1.4.2 Types of mechanical finishes, with examples

Name	Process	Finish	Example uses
Brushing/raising	Fabric is passed through a raising machine. Rollers covered with small wire hooks tease out one end of individual fibres, making them stand up. The other end remains twisted within the staple yarn so that the fibres are not completely detached. Brushing is permanent and weakens a fabric. Brushed fabrics ignite more readily.	Gives a fabric a brushed or napped (hairy) appearance. Improves a fabric's ability to trap air, making it warmer and softer.	Brushed cotton nightwear, shirting. Cotton flannelette bedding. Brushed wool coating and suiting. Polyester fleece garments and accessories.

Name	Process	Finish	Example uses
Calendaring	Fabric is fed through rotating, heated rollers. By rotating at different speeds and by using different types of rollers, different degrees of lustre and effects can be created. Calendaring two ribbed fabrics together creates a moiré effect – a distinctive watermark pattern with lustrous and matt effects.	Produces a smooth, lustrous appearance on the surface of a fabric. Compacts the surface of a fabric by closing the gaps created by warp and weft yarns, making it less penetrable by air and water.	Furnishing fabric such as cotton chintz. Silk, rayon and polyester moiré fabrics used for garments and soft furnishings. Polyester sails for sail boats.
Embossing	Embossing is a type of calendaring process. A pattern is stamped into the fabric as it is passed through heated, engraved rollers. The finish is permanent when heat-set into fabrics made of **thermoplastic** fibres.	Creates raised or sunken patterns and textures on fabrics. Simulates a grain texture on synthetic leather products.	Thermoplastic fabrics, polyester, polyamide. Resin-treated fabrics, e.g. cotton. Furnishing fabrics and some clothing.
Heat-setting	The fabric is stretched to its correct dimensions and held flat before passing through a stenter machine. The heated chamber heat-sets the fabric into shape using the fabric's thermoplastic qualities. When cool the fabric retains the set size and shape. It will not shrink and will crease only if the fabric is washed at too high a temperature.	Improves dimensional stability to stop fabric shrinkage and creasing. Enables a range of functional and aesthetic properties, e.g. a textured, pleated finish.	Thermoplastic fabrics, e.g. polyester, or blends containing at least 60% polyester. Fashion and furnishing products. Socks heat-set into the shape of the foot.
Stone and sand washing (A-level only)	Finished garments or lengths of fabric are placed in industrial washing machines filled with pumice stones or sand. The contents are rotated. The stones or sand buff the fabric, giving it a soft peach-skin texture. It is a permanent finish that can weaken a fabric. Chemical **enzyme** treatments give a similar stonewashed effect.	Adds a worn, aged appearance to fabrics. Gives a soft, flexible handle to fabrics.	Denim for jeans, garments and interior products. Cotton canvas for sails, tents, backpacks. Linen for bedding.

Key terms

Thermoplastic: a material that becomes soft and mouldable above a specific temperature and solidifies upon cooling.

Enzyme: a substance produced by a living organism, which acts as a catalyst to bring about a specific biochemical reaction.

Chemical finishes

Chemical finishes improve the aesthetic qualities and functionality of fabrics by modifying a fibre's structure or a fabric's surface.

Chemical finishes are wet processes involving chemicals, heat and occasionally water. They are applied in a uniform manner using a range of immersion, rolling or spraying techniques.

Table 1.4.3 Types of chemical finishes, with examples

Finish	Process	Example fabrics and uses
Flame retardancy	The chemicals in Proban or Pyrovatex modify fibres by trapping a polymer within the fibres. Chemically treated fabrics will degrade and char. Flame-retardant finishes make fabrics stiff and reduce strength. They are expensive and need careful washing.	Cotton, linen, viscose, rayon. Uses: soft furnishings, nightwear, personal protective clothing.
Water resistance	Two common finishes are Scotchgard and Teflon. Scotchgard is silicone based and is used in furnishing fabrics and carpets. Teflon is PTFE-based. It does not affect the breathability or handle of fabrics, making it ideal for garments such as school uniforms.	All fabrics. Uses: outdoor products (tents, raincoats, tarpaulins), carpets, furniture, shoes, school uniforms.
Non-iron/crease resistance	Fabrics made from cellulosic fibres crease easily during wear and laundering. Synthetic, resin-based chemicals are used to modify the fibres. The treated fabric is held in tension in a heat chamber to **cure** and seal the finish.	Cotton, linen, viscose. Uses: clothing, bedding, soft furnishings. A fabric finished with Teflon is easier to iron.
Shrink resistance	The more a fibre swells when absorbing water, the greater the fabric shrinkage. Synthetic, resin-based chemicals are used to modify the fibres.	Cotton, linen, viscose. Uses: clothing, bedding, soft furnishings.
Moth proofing	The presence of sulphur molecules in wool fibres attracts moths. Impregnating the wool fibres with Mitin or Dielmoth makes the wool fibres inedible to moths without damaging the fabric.	Wool. Uses: blankets, clothing.
Anti-pilling	Polymers or solvents can bind fibres into the surface of a fabric to stop them becoming loose. Biopolishing is an enzyme finish that removes protruding fibres from a fabric's surface.	Wool, cotton, viscose, blended fibre fabrics. Uses: clothing, jumpers.
Hygienic (sanitised)	To give a permanent finish to manufactured fibres, **anti-microbial** chemicals are added directly into the spinning solution or they can be applied to the surface of a fabric. **Anti-bacterial** finishes such as **chitosan** are useful for sensitive skin and allergies. It can be applied as a surface finish or as a microencapsulated finish Cotton fabrics can be treated with an odour-reducing finish called Purista.	Synthetics, regenerated fibres, cotton. Uses: socks, underwear, sportswear, hospital/medical textiles, bedding, catering textiles.

Finish	Process	Example fabrics and uses
	The anti-microbial properties of silver also help control harmful bacteria when added as particles to synthetic yarns.	
Mercerisation (A-level only)	Chemical treatment to make cotton shinier, stronger and more absorbent, improving dye uptake. Cotton yarn or fabric is treated in a concentrated solution of caustic soda. The chemicals cause the cotton fibres to swell and become smoother and more rounded.	Cotton. Uses: sewing thread, garment and furnishing fabric.
Anti-felting (A-level only)	Chemical treatment to prevent felting and shrinkage in animal hair products. Heat and moisture cause the fibres to swell and shrink. Mechanical action (rubbing) causes the scales on the swollen fibres to entangle and interlock, and stops them returning to their original state. To make wool easy-care and machine washable, a Teflon coating can be applied to the surface of the fabric. Synthetic polymers can also be used to coat the surface of fibres, making them smoother so they cannot lock together as easily. Wool treated in this way is called Superwash wool.	Wool, cashmere, angora, mohair. Uses: blankets, jumpers, shawls.

Key terms

Cure: a heat process used to fix dyes and chemical finishes on fabrics.

Anti-microbial: kills or inhibits the growth of microorganisms.

Anti-bacterial: prevents the development of bacteria.

Chitosan: a naturally sourced anti-bacterial found in the shells of crustaceans such as crabs.

Laminating as a finishing process

REVISED

Laminated fabrics are made up of two or more very thin layers of fabric. The layers are held together with adhesives or fused together by heat-setting if thermoplastic fabrics are used.

Gore-Tex

- The Gore-Tex membrane is laminated between a high-performance fabric, for example nylon, and a softer inner lining layer.
- The membrane is a very thin, non-woven polytetrafluoroethylene (PTFE) film with billions of microscopic holes.
- The holes are too small for rainwater to pass through and the membrane acts as a wind barrier, making it totally waterproof and windproof.
- It is breathable as the holes are big enough to let water molecules from perspiration pass through.
- The laminated fabric is lightweight and compact.
- Gore-Tex clothing and footwear is used in a variety of sports and leisure activities, and is also worn by outdoor workers and the emergency services.

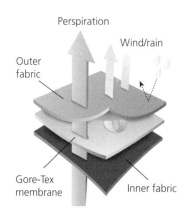

Figure 1.4.1 How Gore-Tex fabric works

Sympatex

- Laminated fabrics with a Sympatex membrane replicate the same waterproof, windproof and breathable properties as Gore-Tex.
- The key difference is that Sympatex polyester membranes are poreless and **hydrophilic** (water-attracting).
- The Sympatex membrane attracts, draws and holds moisture away from the body to transport it to the outside so it can evaporate.
- The poreless membrane structure prevents rain from getting through.

Bonded fabrics (A-level only)

Bonded fabrics are made by laminating a top fabric to a lightweight, woven backing fabric. This improves a fabric's stability and strength without spoiling its handle or appearance, for example PVC faux leather fabric.

> **Typical mistake**
>
> Don't write in general terms. If asked about finishes that can be applied to a specific fabric, keep your examples relevant and appropriate to that fabric. Aim to include modern finishes, as appropriate, in your answer.

Now test yourself

TESTED

1 List four reasons why fabric finishes are used.
2 Explain why designers have to carefully consider whether they should recommend the use of fabric finishes on products they have designed.
3 Give two examples why some finishing processes can have negative effects on fabrics.
4 What is the difference between calendaring and embossing?
5 Explain how a Gore-Tex membrane differs from a Sympatex membrane in laminated fabrics.

1.5 Enhancement of materials

Surface decoration – dyeing

REVISED

The process of dyeing involves three stages:

1 immersing a fabric in soluble **dyestuff**
2 the dye attaching itself to the fabric through absorption or a reaction with the fibres
3 fixing the dye so that the colour remains fast in the fabric.

Vat, discharge and resist dyeing

Vat dyeing

Dyeing on a large scale is done in dye-baths called vats.

- The vats are filled with **dye liquor** and the fabric is dyed in batches.
- The fabric is agitated in the vat to ensure an even dye penetration.
- Excess dye is removed and the fabric is washed with detergents and dried.
- Washing helps to avoid later colour loss.

> **Key term**
>
> **Hydrophilic:** having a strong attraction for water, i.e. water-loving.

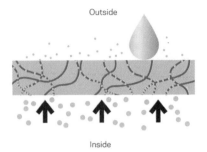

Outside

Inside

Figure 1.4.2 How Sympatex membranes works

> **Exam tip**
>
> Know the specific names and categories of fabric finishes and how they are applied. For different finishes know the classification of fibre they can be used on and be able to give a range of product examples. Be able to discuss the advantages and disadvantages designers and manufacturers face when deciding whether to apply finishes to fabrics.

> **Key terms**
>
> **Dyestuff:** an organic or inorganic coloured substance used to add colour to textile materials.
>
> **Dye liquor:** a solution containing dyestuff, water and chemicals (if needed to help the dye bind to fibres).

Discharge dyeing

Discharge dyeing removes colour from a dyed fabric using a colour-destroying deactivator that bleaches out white or light patterns on the darker coloured background.

Resist dyeing

Resist dyeing creates patterns by preventing colour from going onto certain areas of a fabric.

Traditional hand-finished techniques include:

- **Tie-dye:** wrapped, folded and tied areas on a fabric make it difficult for the dye to be absorbed there. Multi-coloured patterns can be achieved if the fabric is untied after each colour and retied and dyed with new colours. Exact patterns cannot be replicated, making each product an original.
- **Batik:** melted wax or paste is hand-painted onto fabric using a tjanting tool or brush. Once dried the painted areas prevent the dye from going into the fabric. The fabric can be submerged in a dye bath or it can be stretched on a frame and painted with dyes. The wax or paste is then removed.

When dye is applied

Dyes can be applied at all different stages in the processing of textiles.

Table 1.5.1 Applying dyes to fibres, yarns, fabrics and finished products

Dope or spin dyeing	Man-made fibres are coloured before **fibre extrusion**. The dye is added to the spinning solution/dope, making it part of the fibre. This gives the finished fibres excellent light and wash fastness.
Stock dyeing	Fibres, also known as stock, can be dyed before they are spun into yarn.
Yarn dyeing	The yarn is dyed before construction into woven or knitted fabrics. Dyed yarn enables the production of multi-coloured, patterned fabrics such as stripes, checks and **jacquards**. Dyeing at this early stage commits a manufacturer to a fabric colour.
Piece or fabric dyeing	Manufacturers can hold **greige** fabric (undyed, woven or knitted **loomstate** fabric) and dye it as needed to respond to changing fashion styles and colour trends. This is the most commonly used stage as it enables **just-in-time (JIT)** processing.
Garment dyeing	Finished fashion garments can be dyed. A colour can be chosen at this very last stage, enabling retailers and manufacturers to react rapidly to market trends.

Dye fastness

Fabric is considered colourfast if the dyes do not **degrade**, for example by fading, crocking or bleeding, when washed or used. Fabrics need to have **dye fastness** to some or all of the following:

- **Washing:** dye can 'bleed' from fabric when wet.
- **Bleaching:** chlorine bleach can remove colour from most fabrics so dyes used in swimwear need to be resistant to chlorine.
- **Dry cleaning:** the solvents used can cause some dyes to fade.
- **Perspiration:** a reaction to acids in sweat causes colour loss in localised areas such as under the arms.

Key terms

Fibre extrusion: the process where fluid, molten, man-made fibre polymer (dope) is pushed through the holes in the nozzle part of a spinning machine to create filament fibres.

Jacquard fabrics: fabrics where the pattern is created through weaving or knitting rather than being printed onto the fabric.

Greige or **loomstate:** terms used for a fabric in its natural state as it comes from the loom or the knitting machine.

Just-in-time (JIT): a stock-control management system that ensures fabrics and components arrive at the factory just as they are needed to go onto the production line.

Degradation: the gradual breakdown of a dye, leading to loss of colour in a product.

Dye fastness: the ability of a fibre or fabric to retain dye.

- **Toiletries and cosmetics:** chemicals used in deodorants and perfumes can cause discolouration.
- **Light:** dye degrades and fades if repeatedly exposed to strong, bright sun or artificial light.
- **Rubbing (crocking):** abrasion can cause dye loss or colour transfer when the dry, dyed fabric rubs against a lighter coloured fabric.

Dyeing in response to seasonal trends and consumer demands (A-level only)

Seasonal trends

- Colour forecasters analyse sales figures and consumer interest to predict seasonal colour trends.
- Dye companies buy trend information so they can supply the demand for new colours up to two years in advance of a retail season.
- New colour trends are shown to the fashion and textile industry at biannual trade fairs such as Première Vision Yarns and Fabrics.

Consumer demands

- Dyeing fabric at the last stage possible and using just-in-time (JIT) stock control systems gives manufacturers the opportunity to respond quickly to changes in consumer demand.
- JIT production makes products as needed; it is cost-effective and better for the environment as there is less waste.
- Piece fabrics can be kept in their greige state and dyed as needed.
- Simple-shaped garments can be manufactured and kept undyed then dyed to order.

Surface decoration – printing

REVISED

Printing designs on fabrics differs from dyeing in that:
- printed designs do not fully penetrate through a fabric, giving it an identifiable right and wrong side
- the printing medium contains dyes mixed with a thickener to make a viscous paste
- heat processes are the most common method of permanently fixing the dye to a printed fabric.

The main advantages of printing over dyeing are:
- more colours can be used
- complicated designs can be produced
- it is better for the environment as less water is used.

Preparing fabric for printing (A-level only)

To make fabric suitable for printing, it must undergo finishing processes. The steps needed to clean and prepare greige or loomstate fabric for printing, include:
- **Desizing:** the removal of 'size', a water-soluble substance that inhibits the absorption of dye or print medium. Size is applied to warp yarns to strengthen them for the weaving process.
- **Scouring:** the removal of natural or machine impurities such as greases and oils that act as a barrier to dye or print medium absorption.
- **Bleaching:** making the fabric evenly white before colour is added. Synthetic fibres are naturally white so do not require bleaching.

> **Key terms**
>
> **Repeating pattern:** the distance between one point of a design and the exact point where it begins again.
>
> **Photochemically produced screens:** screen's mesh is coated with soluble photosensitive chemicals. Areas to be printed are blocked off to stop them becoming insoluble when exposed to UV light. Washing removes still soluble chemicals from blocked areas; print paste passes through mesh.

Techniques for printing as a surface decoration

The choice of printing technique depends on the amount of fabric to be printed, the print effect required and the budget constraints.

Direct printing (A-level only) prints a design directly onto the fabric using any of the methods shown in Table 1.5.2.

Table 1.5.2 The advantages and disadvantages of surface decoration printing techniques

Technique	Method	Advantages	Disadvantages
Discharge printing (A-level only)	Discharge paste is screen printed onto dyed fabric. The paste destroys the original dye to produce the pattern.	Intricate patterns can be reproduced. Suitable for designs with large areas of background colour. Suitable for large print runs.	Two production stages are involved. Discharge paste is expensive.
Block printing by hand	A design is cut in relief on a wooden block. Printing paste is applied to the block. The block is pressed firmly onto the fabric leaving a **repeating pattern**.	Can be used on any fabrics and fabric sizes. Sustainable as all processes are traditionally done by hand. Blocks can be reused. Gives an ethnic craft aesthetic.	Time consuming and expensive. Accurate positioning is essential. A block is needed for each colour. Only suitable for small-scale runs.
Stencil printing by hand	Gaps are cut into acetate or card to create a pattern. The stencil is positioned on the fabric. Printing paste is sponged or brushed through the cut areas.	Stencils can be cut by hand or laser cutter. Stencils can be reused. Stencilled patterns can entirely cover or enhance small areas of fabrics.	Similar disadvantages to block printing. Suitable only for simple designs with limited colours. Stencils need to be used with care as the sections are connected only with narrow 'bridges'.
Rotary screen printing (Similar to stencilling but the stencils are created as seamless mesh rollers and the process is automated.)	Individual mesh rollers print one colour and part of the repeat design in turn. Designs must fit the rollers seamlessly. The rollers are made by hand using stainless steel mesh, or **photochemically** on woven nylon. The rollers rotate as the fabric travels below on a conveyer belt. An internal squeegee forces printing paste through open mesh areas onto the fabric.	The most commercially viable way of printing large quantities of fabric. Suited to designs that have pattern repeats. Can produce complex designs with five or more colours. CAD is used to prepare the screens. Knitted fabrics can be printed as this method does not stretch the fabric.	Long set-up time. Not suitable for JIT manufacturing. The circumference of the rollers dictates the length of the pattern repeat. Only suitable for high-volume print runs. The initial investment cost for machinery is high.

➜

Technique	Method	Advantages	Disadvantages
Flatbed screen printing (Similar to stencilling but is automated.)	Screens are mesh fabric stretched over frames. Photochemicals create the part design on each screen. A conveyer belt moves and stops the fabric. The screens are lowered, automatic squeegees push printing paste through 'open' areas of the screens. The screens are raised and the fabric moves forward to receive the next colour.	Accurate and relatively fast. Used for high-volume print runs. Good for small-width fabrics. Large screens can print large designs. Can be used on a wider range of fabrics as the number of squeegee passes can be increased. Investment cost is lower than rotary screen printing machinery.	Semi-continuous, stop-start operation. Slower than rotary screen printing. Takes up more factory floor space. Not suitable for JIT production. Not cost-effective for small orders. Better suited to designs with few colours.
Transfer printing/**dye sublimation printing**	CAD generates the design. Long rolls of sublimation paper and inks are used to print the design. The printed paper and white fabric are held together in a heat press. High temperature causes the printed dyes to turn into vapour, transfer and bond with the fabric.	Quick set-up and turnaround time reduces costs. No colour or design constraints. Colour adjustments can be easily made using CAD. Good **colour fastness** as the dye bonds with the fabric. The design covers the full width of the fabric and does not have to repeat. Fabric retains a soft handle.	Only effective on fabrics with 50% or more synthetic fibre content. Slower than screen printing methods. Slightly creased fabric ruins the transfer print. A range of processes are required to set up a print run.
Digital printing	CAD generates the design. The pattern is sent to an ink jet printer fitted with direct dye printing cartridges. The pattern is printed onto the fabric or simple garment, e.g. a T-shirt.	No colour or design constraints. Colour changes are quick to do. Patterns do not have to repeat. Works on most fabrics. Suitable for JIT production. Rapid turnaround of samples. No minimum print run.	Expensive. Suitable for small print runs. The size of the printer and printable area determines the width of the fabric that can be used.

Typical mistake

If asked to choose a printing technique for a named product, make sure you don't choose an inappropriate method for the volume of printed fabric required. For example, incorrectly choosing digital printing as a method for printing fabric for curtains.

Exam tip

Know the specific names of the dyeing and printing techniques and be able to describe in detail how each technique is carried out.

Key terms

Photochemically produced screens: involve coating a screen's mesh with soluble photosensitive chemicals.

Dye sublimation printing: when heat and pressure turn special dyes from a solid into a gas and then back into solid again once it has transferred from paper and bonded with synthetic fabric.

Colour fastness: the ability of a fibre or fabric to retain dye fastness during manufacturing processes and when washed or exposed to sunlight.

Embroidery

REVISED

Embroidery stitches add colour, texture and pattern to a fabric. Stitch variations can be combined for decorative effect and decorative components can also be stitched into a design.

Hand embroidery

- Embroidery thread comes in a range of thicknesses and needs to be used with the correct size and type of needle.
- Embroidery frames help to hold fabric taut and in place while it is being stitched.
- Designs can be drawn onto water-soluble fabric to provide a template.
- Hand embroidery stitches include:
  - **Flat stitches**, e.g. running, back and satin stitch.
  - **Linked stitches**, e.g. chain stitch and feather stitch.
  - **Looped stitches**, e.g. blanket stitch and fly stitch.
  - **Knotted stitches**, e.g. French knots.

Machine embroidery

Pre-programmed stitches

- Most sewing machines are programmed with decorative stitches that can be selected by changing the stitch pattern, length and width dials.
- Computerised sewing machines are pre-programmed with a bigger repertoire of decorative stitches. They also have the ability to stitch pre-programmed motifs, letters and numbers.
- Computerised embroidery machines only sew pre-programmed designs. They come with software that allows users to create their own embroidery designs.
- An attachable embroidery hoop holds the fabric in tension and moves, as programmed, to automatically sew the design.

Free machine embroidery

- Drawing with stitches requires the attachment of a special sewing machine foot.
- Specialist threads such as Madeira thread should be used and lightweight fabrics should be supported with interfacing.
- The fabric must be held taut in a hoop or held flat on the base of the machine.
- The **feed dogs** must be lowered to achieve free motion when embroidering.
- Moving the fabric around, as the machine sews, allows stitches to build up in areas to create unique designs.

Figure 1.5.1 Pre-programmed stitches

> **Key term**
>
> **Feed dogs:** the metal teeth-like ridges that move in and out of the metal plate below a sewing machine's needle and presser foot.

Quilting

REVISED

Quilting adds warmth, structure, pattern and texture to a fabric.

English quilting makes a thick decorative fabric that offers a wearer some protection but more importantly traps air and acts as an insulator. English quilting involves placing a layer of wadding between two layers of fabric and then stitching through the layers using a sewing machine quilting foot. The fabrics should have the grain line running in the same direction and the layers should be pinned and tacked together starting in the middle and working outwards.

Italian and trapunto quilting are decorative techniques that produce a design in relief. Both techniques use two layers of fabric. In Italian quilting, cord is inserted between parallel lines of stitching to create a design. In trapunto quilting, padding is inserted through slits on the underside of small-enclosed stitched areas and then sewn up.

Now test yourself

TESTED

1 What is the difference between vat dyeing and discharge dyeing?
2 List the five different stages when dye can be applied to textiles.
3 Explain what is meant by the terms 'dye fastness' and 'colour fastness'.
4 What factors must manufacturers consider when deciding on which printing technique to use?
5 Use labelled diagrams to show the difference between flatbed and rotary screen printing.

1.6 Modern industrial and commercial practice

Scales of production

REVISED

Manufacturers consider the product type, the number of items to be made and the speed of delivery when deciding which production system to use.

One-off production

One-off production is sometimes called job, individual, make through or **bespoke** production. It refers to individually designed and manufactured products that meet a client's personal specification such as:
- a custom-made suit or dress finished to a very high standard
- a theatre costume
- **haute couture** garments.

One-off production is costly due to:
- the complexity of design, decoration and the use of high-quality fabrics
- fewer economies of scale, for example no bulk discount on materials
- high labour costs – one highly skilled person usually makes the product and this can take days
- the need for high levels of quality control throughout the whole process.

Batch production

Batch production runs are more efficient as teams of workers, skilled in more than one job, work together to make a set number of identical products.
- A batch can range from two to more than 100,000 items, making products cheaper as bulk purchasing of fabrics and components is possible.
- The manufacturing set-up can be altered and teams of workers can simultaneously work on different products.
- Products are less complex in their design and use standardised components.
- Planned quality control checks can be done by checking a specified number of products from each batch.

> ### Key terms
>
> **Bespoke products:** products designed and manufactured to individual specifications.
>
> **Haute couture:** high-end fashion that is constructed by hand from start to finish, and made from top-quality materials and components.

Figure 1.6.1 A tailor making a bespoke suit for an individual client

Examples of batch-produced products include:

- seasonal products such as fashion tops and shorts
- ready-to-wear (**prêt-à-porter**) ranges
- textile merchandise produced for a specific event such as the Olympic Games.

Mass/line production

Mass production systems are set up to continuously manufacture large numbers of identical products over a long period of time.

- The set-up is inflexible and initially expensive. It takes a long time to change if the product is changed and one problem can halt the whole production line.
- Planned quality control checks at key stages are essential to avoid costly mistakes later on.
- Workers become skilled in just one part of the manufacture. Computer aided manufacture (CAM) is used as much as possible to cut labour costs.
- Bulk buying of fabrics and components results in a very low unit cost per item.

Examples of mass-produced products include:

- classic products that never go out of fashion such as Levi's jeans
- items that are in continual demand such as standard white work or school shirts
- simpler, untailored products such as T-shirts.

Line production refers to the linear nature of most production lines where product manufacture is carefully planned so work flows efficiently through a factory in a straight line.

Examples of line production include:

- **Progressive bundle production:** each worker receives a bundle of unfinished garments and performs a single manufacturing process on each garment before the bundle is moved forward to the next worker.
- **Synchronised or straight-line production:** similar to progressive bundle production but one person performs one task on one product before it is moved on. The delivery of work to the workstations is synchronised, meaning products spend exactly the same time at each workstation.
- **Continual flow production:** used for high-volume products where the line runs continuously and never shuts down. It is highly automated and used to produce simple items very cheaply.

Quick response manufacturing

Quick response manufacturing (QRM) is used to reduce product **lead times**. It relies on the rapid transfer of accurate information from the **electronic point of sale (EPOS)** so that batches of products, in the required sizes and colours, can be delivered from stock or made to order in a very short time.

Small teams or production cells/modules complete products from start to finish by sharing tasks and equipment set out in a horseshoe arrangement.

The benefits include:

- faster productivity, efficiency and a motivated workforce
- a reduction in the cost of keeping large volumes of stock
- a fast changeover to supply the ever-changing fashion retail scene and the need for short-run manufacturing.

Key term

Prêt-à-porter: ranges of designer clothes sold ready to wear rather than made to measure.

Key terms

Quick response manufacturing (QRM): a manufacturing strategy that reduces lead times, enabling manufacturers to respond quickly to market demands when manufacturing small numbers of identical products.

Lead time: the time between the start and completion of a production process.

Electronic point of sale (EPOS): a self-contained electronic checkout that accepts all forms of payment, and also updates stock levels.

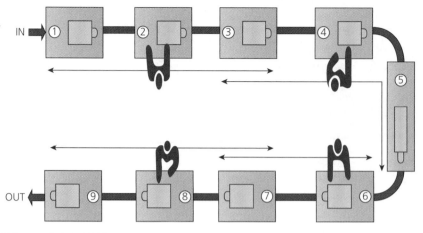

Figure 1.6.2 QRM modular production system

Unit production systems (A-level only)

Unit production systems (UPS) are garment manufacturing systems where the unit of production is a complete product. Computers plan, control, set the rate of delivery and direct the flow of work as the garment is transported to operators via a computer-controlled overhead hanging system.

- The sections of the product are loaded onto a hanging carrier and brought via the overhead conveyor as close to the operator as possible.
- The system is ergonomically designed to minimise handling of the garment and movement needed to position the item to be stitched.
- On completion, the operator presses a button and the carrier moves the product to the next workstation.
- Each garment is tracked within the system and quality control problems can be traced back to the operator.

Installation is costly initially and workers may need specialist training but UPS is cost- and time-efficient because:

- it allows a quick response to market demands, and different styles can be manufactured simultaneously
- labour costs are reduced as there is no handling of bundles
- problems are immediately obvious
- it provides high levels of quality as the garments are hung at each stage of manufacture
- space is used effectively and the total workload of the factory can be balanced efficiently.

Section production (A-level only)

Section production is a development of one-off production; the difference is that the operator specialises in one section of a product.

- The workers are versatile and are able to carry out a number of different processes.
- The factory is organised according to the different sections needed for the garment.
- This system reduces cost and is a very efficient way of producing a variety of styles in reasonable quantities.

Vertical in-house production (A-level only)

Vertical in-house production is where retailers do their own designing, manufacturing and distribution.

> **Key term**
>
> **Unit production system (UPS):** a computerised overhead transportation system that moves garment components automatically from one workstation to the next according to a pre-determined sequence.

- This system minimises the need for external suppliers, and reduces the risks and costs associated with outsourcing manufacture.
- Quality assurance strategies are easier to implement.
- Lead times are more controllable, enabling products to get to the shop floor more quickly.
- Large high-street retailers such as Marks & Spencer and Zara operate this system.

Use of computer systems

REVISED

The fashion industry is reliant on computer-integrated systems to help with designing, manufacturing, distribution and stock control.

Computerised manufacturing systems

Just-in-time

Just-in-time (JIT) is a stock-control management system that is highly dependent on integrated computer systems so that the right materials and finished goods are always available when required.

- Products and stock are tracked using barcodes, which gives manufacturers access to up-to-date stock information.
- JIT saves on storage, monitors output, and stops materials and energy from being wasted on unwanted products.
- It enables high-street fashion stores to react to customers' requirements, enabling them to remain competitive.
- Short-run manufacturing is a form of JIT manufacture.
- A disadvantage of JIT is the system's dependence on reliable suppliers and transport infrastructure.

Modular/cell production (A-level only)

Workers operate in small teams to enable products to be made as QRM, as explained on page 55.

Flexible manufacturing systems (A-level only)

Examples of flexible manufacturing systems include:

- Quick response manufacturing (see page 55).
- Demand activated manufacture: a system that caters for smaller orders of products that are specially tailored to consumers' needs, for example skiwear for a school ski team.
- Demand-based flow (used by online retailers): manufacturers factor production time into an acceptable delivery time so they can produce goods as they are ordered. This system is based on demand–pull rather than schedule–push manufacturing.
- Mass customisation: the modification of standard designs to individual customers' requirements, for example customised trainers.

The use of computer-controlled systems in production, distribution and storage

Figure 1.6.3 shows the extent to which **computer-integrated manufacture (CIM)** can aid production in the textile industry.

- Distribution services are reliant on computerisation to provide **electronic data interchange (EDI)** linkage with suppliers and customers.

> **Key terms**
>
> **Computer-integrated manufacture (CIM):** the term used to describe how computers are used to oversee all stages of bringing a product to market.
>
> **Electronic data interchange (EDI):** a system that allows computers to exchange information electronically in a standard format between business partners.

- In-house departments or specialist companies organise the logistics of storage and distribution using fully computerised warehousing facilities and customised vehicles.
- A JIT stock-control system controlled by EDI barcode systems tracks the progress of the products through the manufacturing and distribution stages.
- Fashion products can also go straight from the factory to the retailer, with no necessity for warehouse storage.
- Computers can collate collections and deliveries, helping to reduce transportation costs and environmental impact.

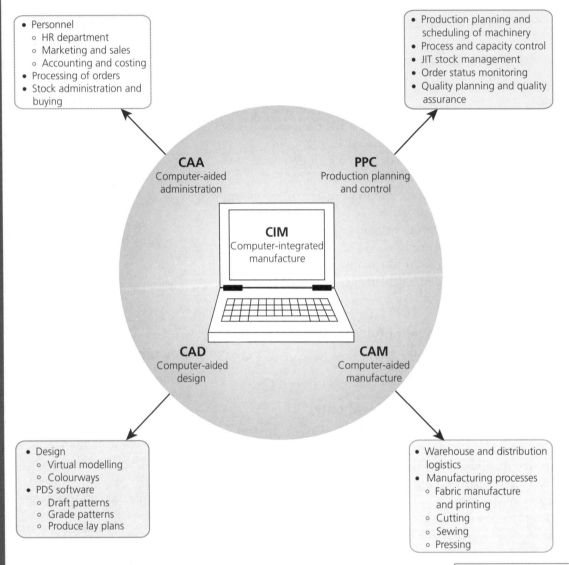

- Personnel
  - HR department
  - Marketing and sales
  - Accounting and costing
- Processing of orders
- Stock administration and buying

- Production planning and scheduling of machinery
- Process and capacity control
- JIT stock management
- Order status monitoring
- Quality planning and quality assurance

CAA
Computer-aided administration

PPC
Production planning and control

CIM
Computer-integrated manufacture

CAD
Computer-aided design

CAM
Computer-aided manufacture

- Design
  - Virtual modelling
  - Colourways
- PDS software
  - Draft patterns
  - Grade patterns
  - Produce lay plans

- Warehouse and distribution logistics
- Manufacturing processes
  - Fabric manufacture and printing
  - Cutting
  - Sewing
  - Pressing

Figure 1.6.3 Computer-integrated manufacture (CIM)

Standardised and bought-in components

Standardised components, such as zip lengths or bias binding widths, come in pre-set sizes and are mostly bought in from specialised manufacturers. Using bought-in components has several advantages:

- There is a wide range to choose from.
- Components can bought in bulk to reduce unit cost.
- JIT stock-control systems can buy components as and when needed.
- Efficient use is made of manufacturing systems as machines are programmed to deal with the pre-set sizes.
- There is no need to invest in machinery to make components.

Key terms

Computer-aided administration (CAA): systems used to plan and carry out all aspects of administration.

Production planning and control (PPC): a system used to plan and control all aspects of manufacturing including quality control.

Sub-assembly

`REVISED`

Some parts of a product can be made as a separate line of manufacture, for example shirt collars or sleeves. The **sub-assembled** parts are then fed into the main production line at the appropriate stage of manufacture.

- The sub-assembly lines do not have to be in the same factory or operated by the same manufacturer.
- Concurrent manufacture can improve product quality, and simplify and speed up the manufacturing process.
- Manufacturers can access specialised machinery or skilled workers without having to invest capital in plant or train workers.
- Sub-assembly facilitates JIT manufacture as product parts can be bought in as needed.

Key term

Sub-assembly: a self-contained, separately manufactured element incorporated in a final product's assembly.

Typical mistake

Don't confuse sub-assembly systems with line manufacture; make it clear that sub-assembly involves separate assembly lines for smaller parts before the product is finally put together.

Global production (A-level only)

`REVISED`

Advances in manufacturing technology and electronic communication have made it easy for companies to trade globally. For example:

- Computerised product data can be emailed across the globe and fed into a company's CIM system, enabling it to make the product within hours of receiving the data.
- Giant contract manufacturing companies in countries like China are set up to make products for different brands globally. They are technologically organised, have capacity and can respond with speed and quality.

Table 1.6.1 Positive and negative impacts of global production

Global production	Positive impacts	Negative impacts
Offshore production	Cheaper overheads and lenient regulation can make production less expensive.	Environmental concerns over the transportation of goods.
	A large, skilled labour pool is available.	Consumer disapproval of perceived or real unethical working practices.
	Production is closer to raw materials.	Increased unemployment in the UK.
	The lack of investment in the textile industry in the UK means offshore factories are more likely to have up-to-date machinery.	Perpetuates the lack of investment and the decline in the UK textile industry.

→

Global production	Positive impacts	Negative impacts
Imports and exports	International trade agreements allow UK manufacturers to export products to other countries. Overseas outlets owned by UK retailers provide export markets for UK-made products, which include high-value, specialised products such as designer clothing and footwear.	Imported low-cost products have contributed to the decline of the UK textile industry. Politics, trade tariffs and fluctuating exchange rates make it difficult for manufacturers to plan and accurately cost manufacture.
Branded goods	Brands help to sell UK products in the global marketplace. They help to distinguish one designer or retailer from another. They give some legal protection from competitors if registered as a trademark. When consumers trust a brand or like the lifestyle image it conveys, they become loyal and buy more.	It is expensive to set up and maintain a brand name. Negative events such as bad press (e.g. Nike's use of sweatshops) or controversial advertising campaigns (e.g. Benetton) are more easily attached to brands. The brand can make high-value products attractive to counterfeiters.
Contracted goods	Contractors, usually located in developing countries, can set up high-volume production runs to make products at a low unit cost. Retailers do not have to invest in their own manufacturing facilities or workforce. Retailers can use contractors to produce pilot runs of products for test marketing purposes. Contractors give retailers an operational advantage as short-term increases in demand can be met by hiring additional production capacity.	Consumer disapproval of retailers profiting from perceived or real exploitative labour in sweatshops. Retailers increase the risk of losing sensitive commercial or technical information by working with contractors who may also make products for their competitors. Environmental concerns over the transportation of goods.

Now test yourself

TESTED

1 Name the factors that influence a manufacturer's choice of production system.
2 What level of quality control is needed for one-off, batch and mass production?
3 What term is used to describe the organisation of manufacturing to reduce the need to rely on external suppliers?
4 List three reasons why manufacturers buy in standardised components made by specialist manufacturers.
5 Discuss the advantages and disadvantages of contract manufacture for the retailers of fashion products.

1.7 Digital design and manufacture

Computer-aided design (CAD)

REVISED

Advantages and disadvantages

Table 1.7.1 Using CAD compared to hand-generated alternatives

Advantages	Disadvantages
• CAD can save time and money, and improve accuracy. • Designs can be edited rather than drawn by hand from scratch for each iteration.	• The initial set-up costs are high. • The client, designer and manufacturer all need to have compatible IT systems.
• Experimental changes can be made quickly on screen. • **Pattern design systems (PDS)** can draft and grade pattern pieces, produce **lay plans** and send the information to a computer-integrated, automated cutting system. • Virtual modelling software replaces the need to hand-make physical samples, which has less impact on the environment. • Designs and developments are more accurate. Pattern pieces can be retrieved from a database and printed out in pristine condition.	• The systems require regular updates and technical support. • There is the potential for cyber attacks.

Key terms

Pattern design system (PDS): a computer program that makes pattern templates automatically from a 3D model.

Lay plan: a diagram showing how pattern templates are to be placed onto fabric ready for cutting out.

Developing and presenting ideas

When developing and presenting ideas for products, CAD can be used to:
- generate and accelerate the development of product design and pattern ideas for fabric
- show designs with photorealistic rendering and manipulated scanned artwork
- simulate ideas interactively – 3D models can be viewed from any angle, allowing errors to be detected and corrected at an early stage
- show final ideas on a **presentation board** to collect client and marketing feedback
- present ideas by email, speeding up decision making
- test out the likely cost of a product by manipulating variables in a spreadsheet.

Key term

Presentation board: a collection of illustrations, samples and colourways used to present final ideas to a client.

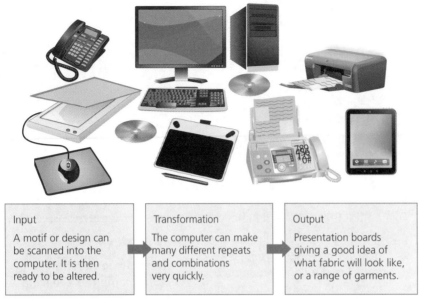

Input	Transformation	Output
A motif or design can be scanned into the computer. It is then ready to be altered.	The computer can make many different repeats and combinations very quickly.	Presentation boards giving a good idea of what fabric will look like, or a range of garments.

Figure 1.7.1 CAD software is used to develop patterns for fabric

Industrial applications (A-level only)

Industrial applications of CAD offer features such as the ability to:

- show ideas in different colourways using a **Pantone** colour palette, **image mapping** or as a **virtual prototype**
- plan and create accurate pattern repeats for printed fabrics
- create accurate pattern templates from 3D models using PDS
- plan accurate and correct lay plans to maximise profit and minimise fabric wastage
- send complex information directly to computer-aided manufacturing (CAM) machines, for example laser cutters and CAM embroidery machines.

> **Key terms**
>
> **Pantone:** a standardised colour matching system.
>
> **Image mapping:** allows a designer to show how a pattern or colour might look on a garment.
>
> **Virtual prototype:** a 3D prototype product modelled on a computer but not actually made.

Figure 1.7.2 The computer can make pattern templates instantly from a 3D model of a garment using PDS

Computer-aided manufacturing (CAM)

REVISED

For CAM machines to work in conjunction with CAD, the CAD files need to be converted into special code using a **computer numerically controlled (CNC)** program.

CAM is often used to replace manual operations because:

- machines can work quickly and continuously

> **Key term**
>
> **Computer numerical control (CNC):** a program, converted from CAD files, which uses special codes to control CAM equipment.

- quality is more consistent as highly specialised machines are programmed to carry out identical operations
- machines can work with materials and chemicals that might be harmful to humans.

Some automated processes will still require manual input, for example picking up sections of the garment and presenting them to the programmed machine for sewing.

CAM processes

Fabric manufacture

Computer-controlled weaving looms are programmed to lift the correct warp yarns to allow the insertion of weft yarns to create different weaves, for example satin weave or fabrics with coloured woven patterns such as checks or brocades.

The main methods used are:
- The gripper system has several gripper-projectiles that take it in turns to launch and carry an individual weft yarn at high speed, in the same direction, across the loom.
- The rapier system has a rod with a gripper that takes the weft to the centre of the loom where a second rod picks it up and carries it to the opposite side.
- Jet systems use water or pressurised air to insert the weft by carrying it across the width of the fabric.

Typical mistake

If asked to describe examples of CAM machinery, make reference to the computer control element and be able to differentiate between standard sewing processes and those that are automated.

Machines, whether computer controlled or not, have been used for many years to carry out industrial processes. The simplistic view that automated systems mean that products no longer need to be sewn by hand will not get you many marks.

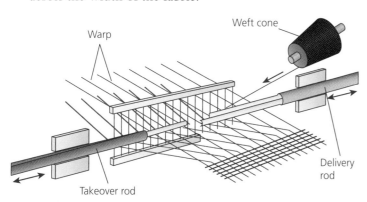

Figure 1.7.3 A rapier system uses two gripper rods to insert the weft

Other CAM machines controlled by computers include:
- weft and warp knitting machines
- circular knitting machines
- highly specialised machines, which produce seamless garments
- jacquard weaving and knitting machines.

Fabric printing

CAD software is used to develop print designs and individual screens for screen printing. CAM usually controls the movement of the fabric, the supply of dye and the movement of the screens.

Further information about these printing techniques can be found in Chapter 1.5, page 51.

Lay planning and computer-controlled cutting

A PDS can produce a lay plan to show how pattern pieces should be placed on the fabric so that:

- there is minimum wastage
- different garment sizes can be cut together to reduce waste
- all the pattern pieces are cut out
- any pattern, one-way design or nap in the fabric is taken into account
- pattern pieces are cut on the correct grain of the fabric.

To save time and money, many layers of fabric are spread and cut out at the same time. Computer-controlled spreading machines guarantee that the fabric edges are laid exactly on top of each other and the patterns on woven or knitted fabric are in the same place on each layer.

- Computer-controlled cutting machines use knives, laser beams and high-pressure water jets.
- Cut-out pieces for a product are put into bundles, labelled with a barcode then sent for sewing.
- Computers read the barcodes and monitor each product's progress throughout manufacture.

Automated buttonholing

Automatic buttonhole machines use CNC machines programmed to accurately space and repeatedly make buttonholes of the same shape and size.

- Computer-controlled button sewing machines automatically sew the pre-programmed stitch patterns for buttons with two or four holes.

Making and sewing of pockets

A profile sewing system uses a jig and a template to automatically place and stitch patch pockets onto garments.

The flat pocket is hemmed at the top edge then fed onto a template and positioned in the exact place it is to be stitched. The edges are automatically folded under and a jig holds the pocket down while the machine stitches it to the garment in a pre-determined pattern.

Seam stitching

An automated CNC profile machine can be programmed to stitch different seam types, for example fell seams in the legs of trousers. A CAM linking machine can join knitted fabrics stitch by stitch to create knitted seams.

Pressing

Computers can control pressing during manufacture and on garment completion.

- Automated conveyor fusing presses are programmed to give an even finishing when fusing interfacing.
- A steam dolly is a specialist-pressing machine that uses steam and air to inflate the inside of clothes, making creases fall out.

Computer-controlled decorative processes

Computer-controlled machines can be used to produce logos and embroidery quickly and accurately using many different coloured threads.

Figure 1.7.4 A computer-controlled pressing machine that can store different pressing programs in its memory

Laser cutting

Lasers can be programmed using CAD software to etch or cut out intricate patterns on most fabrics. The laser seals the edges at the same time as it cuts, stopping edges from fraying.

Virtual modelling (A-level only)

REVISED

Simulation

- Computer software can simulate a proposed production system to check production is possible before changing the layout of a factory or investing in new equipment.
- Simulations can indicate how long it will take to manufacture a product.
- Simulation programs and EPOS information can model sales projections, enabling companies to be ready to react to consumer demand, leading to demand-activated manufacture.

Pattern design systems

- A PDS helps with the design of garments and the development of pattern templates.
- It can also be used to present images and virtual prototypes to clients as it can simulate fabric texture, drape and garment fit on realistic, virtual body forms.
- It can be used to create a customised fit using data from 3D **body scanners** or measurements taken by hand, so a customer can see how a garment might look and drape on their body.

> **Key term**
>
> **Body scanner:** captures measurements and the shape of a customer's body to produce a highly accurate 3D digital body form.

Computer-controlled printing to produce sample fabric lengths

- Digital printing allows designers to quickly test out fabric designs by printing short lengths of fabric directly from a CAD program.
- Physical samples help designers check the print works with a fabric's surface texture and weight.

Electronic data interchange (A-level only)

REVISED

Electronic data interchange (EDI) is a system that relies on the use of computers to electronically exchange all documents.
- EDI networks analyse consumer trends and use the information to meet consumer demand.
- Companies with computerised warehousing facilities use EDI to link and monitor distribution to suppliers and customers.

The textile industry uses barcodes to represent data about a product. **EPOS** is a computer-based scanned barcode system used to read barcode information as well as capture data when products are purchased. The advantages of an EPOS system are:
- stock levels are easily monitored and the system automatically reorders if stock levels are low or a particular colour or size is out of stock
- **demand-activated manufacture** is more sustainable as there is no over-production of products
- it saves money as shops do not need storage facilities
- sales data and customer details are collected for use by marketing departments to inform the development of new products and marketing strategies.

> **Key terms**
>
> **Electronic data interchange (EDI):** a system that allows computers to exchange information electronically in a standard format between business partners.
>
> **Electronic point of sale (EPOS):** a self-contained electronic checkout that also updates stock levels.
>
> **Demand-activated manufacture:** uses digital technology to produce fashion products on demand as customers order them.

Production, planning and control (PPC) networking (A-level only)

REVISED

Computers in a PPC network plan and control all aspects of manufacturing. This can be particularly useful in the fashion industry, which has complex production networks that can span different businesses and cross international boundaries.

The advantages of PPC networking include:

- centrally stored information, which allows for improved decision making and control, enabling companies to respond quickly when circumstances change
- improved control of 'in-time' availability in the supply of materials and components, which reduces costly hold-ups in production
- more efficient planning of processes and machine requirements
- the ability to manage capacity and allocate orders
- efficient planning for style changeovers
- fewer production stoppages and more efficient production performance, which reduces late delivery penalties
- the ability to constantly monitor the flow of production and see the status of all orders
- the ability to track orders throughout the supply chain and to deal quickly with transport and delivery issues

Availability of materials

PPC systems are used to coordinate different delivery dates to ensure that all materials and components are available using a JIT system. These systems keep track of what has been ordered and when it will be delivered.

Scheduling of machines and people

PPC systems are used to plan production schedules, to ensure the machines and trained operatives needed to make a specific product are available.

Potential bottlenecks during the manufacture of a product can be identified and a production plan can be produced that allocates extra machines and operatives for processes that take a longer time to complete.

The flow of work and work schedules can also be planned throughout the year, helping a company to remain efficient, competitive and able to retain its trained workers.

Coordinating suppliers and customers

With a PPC system it is possible to constantly monitor the status of orders and track orders throughout the supply chain. PPC links to EPOS for demand-activated manufacture and the JIT organisation of materials and components.

> **Exam tip**
>
> Make sure you understand the wider nature of the key electronic systems in modern manufacture. Don't just concentrate on the benefits of CAD and CAM processes, which are only a small part of an integrated system. Include examples that support the design, manufacture, distribution and selling of fashion and textile products. Give details of specific automated manufacturing processes and systems such as JIT, EDI, EPOS and PPC.

Now test yourself

TESTED

1 Give four advantages of CAD over the manual drawing of designs.
2 What is a PDS?
3 Describe three different ways CAM is used to speed up garment manufacture.
4 How do virtual modelling and virtual prototypes differ?
5 Explain how EPOS works and list the types of information represented by barcodes.

1.8 The requirements of textile and fashion design and development

Product development and improvement

In commercial companies, product developers:

- deliver new textile and fashion designs to consumers
- critically analyse designs to address consumer needs and improve existing designs
- critically analyse competitors' ranges to consider incorporating successful features in their own designs
- analyse sales figures to identify their best-selling designs
- update their best-selling designs to give them a fresh appeal and meet forecasted trends.

Product developers use information about the latest trends from trade fairs to make sure they:

- use the next season's predicted fashion colours
- use fabrics, trims and components that are going to be on trend
- incorporate predicted styling details, such as hemline length, and embellishments such as embroidery.

Critical analysis of existing products

Closely studying and **disassembling** a product gives designers and product developers useful information. Consumer reviews and feedback can also inform future product development.

The critical analysis of a product can involve:

- considering the product's intended use and target market
- being objective and factual when aesthetically analysing the product
- analysing the product's ergonomics
- finding out how the product has been constructed and what production processes have been used
- looking at the fabrics used, the suitability of their properties and the construction methods used
- listing the components used, and considering why the designer chose them
- studying the link between the fabrics, method of manufacture and the scale of production
- considering the environmental issues associated with the manufacture, care and use of the product, plus what will happen to it at the end of its life
- considering if there are any social or moral issues related to manufacturing the product.

Design, development and manufacture to meet specification criteria

A **design specification** sets out the criteria for the design of a product. It clearly communicates instructions to the designer and the product development team.

> **Key term**
>
> **Disassembly:** to take apart step-by-step, or to deconstruct.

> **Exam tip**
>
> When critically analysing a product, don't just concentrate on the design weaknesses. Make sure your analysis is objective and includes the positive and desirable features of the product. Include references to the product's intended end user and the environment it is designed for in your answer.

Criteria are usually generic and include:

- function
- aesthetics
- customer
- size
- cost
- materials
- environment
- safety
- timescale.

The **product specification** and **manufacturing specification** are used as a contract to ensure accurate product information is communicated from the product development team to the client's factory. These **specifications** include:

- working drawings (with precise dimensions included)
- details of fabrics, components (including precise amounts)
- details of any decorative techniques
- agreed **tolerances** and seam allowances
- clear description of each production stage
- instructions for quality control checks
- equipment list
- lay plan
- costing
- labelling and packaging information.

A gold seal standard is a sample product taken from the production line and held by the client. It is used along with the specification to check the quality of subsequent products.

Fitness for purpose

To be fit for purpose, a product should look right, work as intended, perform well in use and be within budget.

The design specification is used to ensure all these elements of the design are suitable for the product's requirements.

Accuracy of production (A-level only)

Accuracy is achieved by:

- precisely following the information in the product and manufacturing specifications and by working to agreed tolerance levels
- applying planned quality checks to test samples of the manufactured product at intervals during the production schedule
- using computer-integrated manufacture where possible to eliminate worker error.

Working with a variety of materials

Materials should be suited to a new product's purpose and function but they should also have aesthetic interest and appeal. Some of the ways this can be achieved are by:

- using fabrics with different textures, construction methods and weights within the design
- manipulating the fabric or using heat-setting to add pleats or tucks to give textural effects
- using trims to add pattern, colour and texture
- using beads or sequins to add sparkle and textural contrast and interest
- using components such as novel button styles or other 3D features such as flowers
- using interfacing and wadding to create different textures and 3D effects.

Key terms

Specifications: used to test designs, prototypes and manufactured products.

Tolerance: the acceptable variation in the size or part of a product, usually given as upper and lower limits.

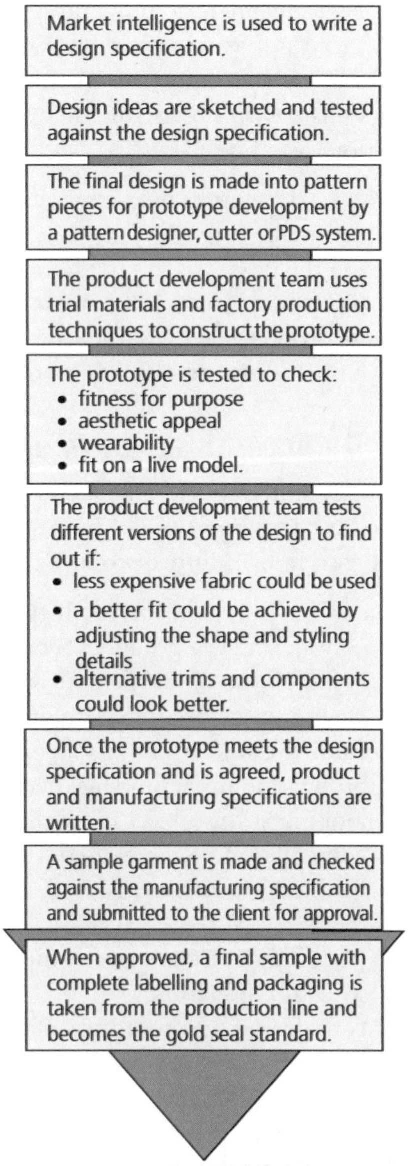

Market intelligence is used to write a design specification.

Design ideas are sketched and tested against the design specification.

The final design is made into pattern pieces for prototype development by a pattern designer, cutter or PDS system.

The product development team uses trial materials and factory production techniques to construct the prototype.

The prototype is tested to check:
- fitness for purpose
- aesthetic appeal
- wearability
- fit on a live model.

The product development team tests different versions of the design to find out if:
- less expensive fabric could be used
- a better fit could be achieved by adjusting the shape and styling details
- alternative trims and components could look better.

Once the prototype meets the design specification and is agreed, product and manufacturing specifications are written.

A sample garment is made and checked against the manufacturing specification and submitted to the client for approval.

When approved, a final sample with complete labelling and packaging is taken from the production line and becomes the gold seal standard.

Figure 1.8.1 Simplified stages in the development of a textile product

---

Aesthetics, ergonomics and anthropometrics

Aesthetics

- **Aesthetics** is concerned with how a product looks, and includes shape, form, symmetry, size, proportion, colour and texture.
- A product's attractive appearance produces pleasant emotions in users and leads to a better user experience.
- Balancing aesthetics and function is central to the commercial success of a product.

Ergonomics

- **Ergonomics** is the study of the ways in which a product, the user and the environment the product is used in affect each other.
- It applies anthropometric data to resolve design issues relating to the ergonomic needs of the user.
- An example is the 'Easy Button'. The shape and size of the button make it easier for people with limited fine motor skills to use independently.

Anthropometrics

- **Anthropometrics** is the study of the sizes of people in relation to products.
- Measurement data is analysed and presented as standards, for example BS 3728 Size designations of children's and infants' wear.
- Anthropometrics helps designers take into consideration the range of sizes and abilities, such as grip capabilities, that exist within humans.

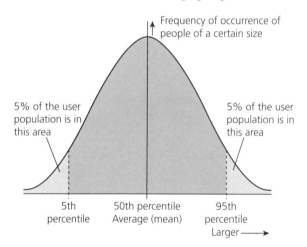

Figure 1.8.3 Percentiles

Inclusive design

REVISED

Inclusive design is about designing products that are accessible to, and usable by, as wide a range of people as possible. This includes groups such as the disabled, children, the elderly, transgender people and gender non-conformists.

- Inclusive designs have to be accessible and attractive without losing aesthetic appeal.
- **Empathic design** can make big improvements in the lives of people who feel they have been excluded because of ageism or because they don't conform to a particular body shape or **gender stereotype**.

> **Key terms**
>
> **Aesthetics:** the beauty or tastefulness of the look of a product, and how attractive it is to the consumer.
>
> **Ergonomics:** the relationship between people and the products they use.

These buttons have been ergonomically designed for elderly people.

Figure 1.8.2 Ergonomic buttons

> **Key terms**
>
> **Anthropometrics:** scientific measurements of the human body applied to the design of products.
>
> **Percentiles:** a specific statistical percentage range, often used to define appropriate anthropometric data for design purposes.

> **Key terms**
>
> **Inclusive design:** designing products for ease of use by the maximum possible range of people.
>
> **Empathic design:** user-centred design approach that considers the user's feelings towards products.

- Fashion advertising campaigns that use realistically shaped models and people from a wider diversity of backgrounds help to break down stereotypes and promote inclusivity.
- Zara's 'Ungendered' and Selfridges' 'Agender' androgynous/gender-neutral ranges use style and colour to challenge gender stereotypes.
- **Adaptive clothing** is clothing designed to be easy to wear for people who experience difficulties dressing independently or need the help of a carer. Ranges from Target and Tommy Hilfiger have the same outward appearance as their typical designs but use magnetic closures, Velcro seams, one-handed zippers and stretch fabrics to ease fit. Other companies produce stylish adaptive clothing that discreetly accommodates or provides easy access for medical equipment, medical procedures, incontinence pads and dressings.

Key terms

Gender stereotypes: over-generalisations about the characteristics of people based on their gender.

Adaptive clothing: products designed to meet the needs of people with poor mobility and dexterity.

Typical mistake

Don't be too general when discussing inclusive design. Illustrate your answer with examples of companies that promote inclusivity or products that have been designed to be inclusive. Make sure your answer addresses the specific needs of as wide a diversity of people as possible. Don't just focus on design issues related to children or the elderly.

Now test yourself

TESTED ☐

1 What is the role of a product developer?
2 List four pieces of information a product developer will look for when analysing a product.
3 What is the name given to the set of key criteria against which a design will be tested?
4 What is the difference between aesthetics, anthropometrics and ergonomics?
5 Explain how clothing can be made more inclusive.

1.9 Health and safety

Employers have a legal obligation to ensure that strict health and safety legislation is implemented. Employees are also required to follow all procedures to eliminate health hazards and prevent accidents to themselves and others.

Good working practices and systems create a safe environment. Lost time through injuries and investigated accidents cost money and could affect the reputation of a business.

Safe working practices

REVISED ☐

The employer or an appointed health and safety officer is responsible for carrying out a range of tasks that help to prevent accidents and injuries. They must ensure the following:

- All equipment, tools and machinery are safe to work with and are fitted with safety guards or emergency stop buttons as appropriate.
- All equipment, tools and machinery are regularly maintained and tested for safety.

Acute toxicity, Very toxic (fatal), Toxic, etc.

Gases under pressure

Harmful skin irritation, serious eye irritation

Flammable gases

Explosive, self reactive, organic peroxide

Harmful to the environment

Oxidising gases, oxidising liquids, oxidising solids

Respiratory sensitiser, mutagen, carcinogen, reproductive toxicity, systemic target organ toxicity, aspiration hazard

Corrosive (causes severe skin burns and eye damage), serious eye damage

Figure 1.9.1 Hazard pictograms

- Training and adequate supervision are provided for all equipment, tools and machinery.
- Ergonomically designed work stations are used.
- Dangerous items and substances are used and stored safely.
- Accident reporting systems are in place, RIDDOR (Reporting of Injuries, Diseases and Dangerous Occurrences Regulations (2013)).
- Welfare facilities such as first aid are provided.
- Adequate breaks are planned for.
- Statutory safety legislation is observed and obeyed.

These practices are designed to keep people safe and free from harm, and are much the same across schools, colleges and industry.

Table 1.9.1 Safe working practices in school/college workshops

• All safety rules and signage must be followed.	• Care must be taken when handling hot liquids such as batik wax.
• Machinery or equipment must not be used unless the operator is supervised or trained in its use.	• All safety guards and safety measures must be used.
• No eating or drinking.	• Breakages or damaged tools or equipment must be reported to a teacher.
• PPE must be worn when using machinery or handling chemicals such as dyes.	• Hands must be kept away from cutting blades.
• Long hair must be tied back to avoid entrapping in machinery.	• The correct operating temperature for equipment such as a batik pot or iron must be checked.
• Work areas and walkways must be kept neat and free of trip hazards.	• Hot or heavy equipment must be operated only on a firm level surface.
• Spillages should be reported.	
• Seats must be adjusted to personal height requirements when operating machinery.	• Hands and fingers must be kept away from moving parts of machines.
• All persons must be aware of the emergency procedures, e.g. fire evacuation routes.	• Electrical equipment must be switched off at the socket after use to avoid injury through accidental operation.
• The correct tools for jobs must be used.	• If a person becomes ill or injured this must be reported to a teacher immediately.

Health and Safety at Work Act 1974

- The **Health and Safety at Work Act (HASAWA) 1974** is the primary piece of legislation covering workplace health and safety in Britain.
- It states that employers (so far as is **reasonably practicable**) must protect the health, safety and welfare of all employees and visitors.
- The act makes it a legal requirement for employers to carry out **risk assessments** and put sensible measures in place to control risk.
- It places an obligation on employees to cooperate and report inadequacies in health and safety arrangements and not to interfere with or misuse anything provided to assure health, safety or welfare at work.
- The **Health and Safety Executive (HSE)** is responsible for enforcing the HSWA.

Key terms

Health and Safety at Work Act (HASAWA) 1974: the primary legislation for British health and safety law.

Reasonably practicable: means balancing the level of risk against the measures needed to control the real risk in terms of money, time or trouble.

Risk assessment: a statutory process that considers what might cause harm to people and what reasonable steps might be taken to prevent that harm.

Health and Safety Executive (HSE): a national independent watchdog for work-related health, safety and illness.

Control of Substances Hazardous to Health Regulations (2002)

- To comply with the **Control of Substances Hazardous to Health Regulations (COSHH)**, employers must carry out risk assessments to prevent, reduce or control their workers' or adjacent workers' exposure to substances that may be hazardous.
- Exposure could cause chronic lung diseases, skin problems, eye irritation or asthma.
- Hazardous textile substances include dyestuffs, bleaches, chemicals used to apply finishes to fabrics, adhesives and cleaning materials.
- Hazardous substances must carry a clear warning label that identifies what the hazard is.

Risk management

- In organisations where there are five or more employees it is mandatory to have a health and safety policy that formally records risk assessments.
- The employer, or a designated health and safety officer, must identify potential **hazards** associated with the manufacturing processes that might cause harm to people.
- If a hazard is identified, the next stages are to assess, control and monitor the associated risk.
- Not all risks can be eliminated, but risk assessments ensure that all reasonable practicable measures are taken to minimise risk and prevent harm.
- Risk assessments are effective only if employees follow them and employers review them regularly.

> ### Key terms
>
> **Control of Substances Hazardous to Health Regulations (COSHH):** legislation to prevent, reduce or control people's exposure to hazardous substances in the workplace.
>
> **Hazard:** a danger or risk that can cause someone harm.

- Consider the likely risks
- Use the results of workplace inspections
- Use incident reports
- Analyse risks of new machinery/equipment
- Analyse risks in new or changed manufacturing processes

- Regularly monitor and review the effectiveness of control measures
- Check whether the situation has changed
- Check whether there are new risks emerging

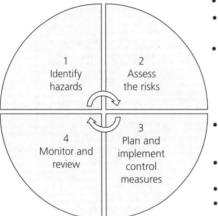

- Use a risk assessment proforma
- Consider how severe the impact of the risk will be
- Rank the risk according to its likelihood of occurring

- Change equipment or materials to remove a hazard
- Isolate people from the hazard
- Improve training
- Change working methods/ systems
- Use PPE
- Set review dates

Figure 1.9.2 Risk assessment cycle

Safety precautions and risk assessment in manufacturing processes (A-level only)

Key term

Safety precautions: actions carried out in advance that protect against a possible danger or injury.

Table 1.9.2 Common risks and safety precautions in textile manufacturing processes

Process	Risk	Safety precautions
Handling heavy rolls of fabric	Back injury from lifting. Foot or head injury if rolls fall from a height.	Use lifting equipment. Provide instruction on the correct way to lift heavy items. Wear PPE: steel toe-cap shoes and hard hat.
Movement of heavy goods around the factory floor	Injury from impact with forklift truck or other vehicle.	Have designated safe zones or walkways. Fit vehicles with flashing lights and/or reverse signal alarms.
Spreading and cutting fabric	Hand/finger injury from machines. Inhalation of dust or dust irritant in eyes.	Use machine safety guards and operate only if trained. Wear PPE: chainmail gloves, breathing mask and safety goggles.
Fusing press, e.g. applying fusible interfacing	Hand/finger injury. Burns from press. Inhalation of unhealthy vapours.	Use presses only if trained. Wear PPE: protective gloves and breathing mask. Know first-aid procedures for burns.
Machine sewing	Hand/finger injury from sharp parts. Hair/clothing entrapment. Eye injury from breaking needles. Back injury.	Ensure needle guards are in place, fit emergency stop buttons. Tie back long hair and wear overalls and safety glasses. Use ergonomically designed workstations and job rotation to avoid repetitive strain injury (RSI) or injury caused by concentration lapses from doing the same task with no variation.
Pressing equipment	Burns or scalds from hot equipment. Finger/hand injury from presses.	Use the equipment and steam presses only if trained. Fit emergency stop buttons on machines. Turn on the steam function only when ready to use. Hand irons must be fitted with a thermostat to protect them from overheating.
Dyeing and printing fabric	Inhalation or eye contact with dyestuff or solvents. Skin damage or reaction to contact with dyes etc.	COSHH safety labelling instructions on containers must be followed. Ensure correct ventilation. Wear PPE: dust mask, safety goggles, protective gloves and overalls. Know first-aid procedures for working with chemicals.

→

Process	Risk	Safety precautions
General working area	Tripping and falling. Electric shocks. RSI injuries. Cuts and pricks from sharp points.	Keep all work areas clear and tidy. Maintain and regularly safety test electrical equipment. Allow the workforce regular breaks. Scissors should be kept in special holders when not in use, and pins and needles kept in containers.
Materials handling	Head injury from overhead conveyor system. Hand/finger injury from conveyors.	Floor area where transporter rails pass must be painted with black and yellow warning stripes. Provide designated safe zones or walkways. Safety guards must be fitted and training in the handling of conveyors given.
Packaging machinery	Hand/finger injury.	Fit emergency stop buttons on machines. Use packaging machinery only if trained.

Safety in products and services to the customer

REVISED

Designers and manufacturers have a responsibility to consider the safety of potential users. Safety legislation and standards are used to protect consumers from poor-quality and unsafe products.

Legislation also protects consumer rights, enabling customers to claim a refund if goods are faulty or do not meet the manufacturer's performance claims.

Legislation used to protect consumers

The enforcement of safety legislation is the responsibility of trading standards officers, who can stop the sale of unsafe products and prosecute the supplier. Laws that relate to the design and manufacture of textile products in the UK include:

- the **General Product Safety Regulations (2005)**
- the **Furniture and Furnishings (Fire Safety Amendment) Regulations (1993)**
- the **Trade Descriptions Act (2011)**.

Safety standards in children's clothing

The BSI and the European Committee for Standardisation (CEN) have produced a **code of practice** for the design and manufacture of children's clothing to promote mechanical safety. Examples include:

- No cords or drawstrings around the hood and neck areas of children aged 0–7 years and, for 7–14 year olds, the maximum length allowed is 75 mm.
- No cords or ribbons accessible to a child's mouth as unraveled fibres could be a choking hazard. The ends of cords or ribbons must be secured through heat-sealing to prevent fraying.
- No loose threads, which could get wrapped around fingers or toes causing a tourniquet effect, restricting blood circulation.
- No zips in trousers for boys under the age of five.
- No components such as buttons that look or smell like food.

> **Key terms**
>
> **General Product Safety Regulations (2005):** place a responsibility on businesses to supply safe goods.
>
> **Furniture and Furnishings (Fire Safety Amendment) Regulations (1993):** set levels of fire resistance for fabric coverings used in upholstered furniture and furnishings.
>
> **Trade Descriptions Act (2011):** makes it an offence for businesses to make false or misleading statements about goods or services.
>
> **Code of practice:** a voluntary set of rules agreed by a professional body that guide a company's way of working.

- No hoods on sleepwear for babies less than 12 months, to prevent overheating.
- A consideration of the restriction in vision and hearing a hood may cause in garments for older children.

Flammability of textiles

Under the Nightwear (Safety) Regulations (1985), it is an offence to supply nightwear (pyjamas, babies' garments and cotton terry towelling bath robes) that does not meet flammability performance regulations set by the BSI.

Nightwear that does not meet the flammability requirements must have a permanent sewn-in label with 'KEEP AWAY FROM FIRE' in red letters.

Nightwear that meets BSI flammability requirements must also have a permanent label that includes one or both of the following:
- 'LOW FLAMMABILITY TO BS 5722' in black letters
- 'KEEP AWAY FROM FIRE' in red letters.

Consumer Rights Act (2015)

The **Consumer Rights Act (2015)** safeguards consumers against faulty products. Part 1 primarily relates to product design and consumer rights:
- Goods are to be of satisfactory quality; commensurate to the price paid.
- Goods are to be fit for purpose.
- Goods are to be as described.

Under the act, consumers have the right to reject and return goods and claim a refund:
- The initial right to reject goods is a 30-day period if the goods do not meet the above terms. This right entitles the consumer to a 100 per cent refund.
- If after 30 days but within 6 months of the purchase date the product becomes defective, the consumer is entitled to claim a repair or replacement.
- If the repair or replacement is unsuccessful, the consumer can claim a price reduction or a final right to reject the goods. The reduction or refund can be up to 100 per cent of the product value.
- Consumers have the right to dispute resolution either through the small claims court or through an ombudsman such as the Citizens Advice Bureau.

These rights do not apply if a consumer simply changes their mind about a product. However, if the product is in good condition and the consumer has proof of purchase, many retailers will refund or give a credit note as a gesture of goodwill.

> ### Key term
>
> **Consumer Rights Act (2015):** an act that simplifies consumer protection law and reflects the changing ways that consumers buy goods and services.

> ### Exam tip
>
> Make sure you can quote legislation that specifically applies to a range of different textile products and be able to describe the purpose of that legislation.

> ### Typical mistake
>
> Don't write in general terms when discussing health and safety and consumer rights legislation. Be able to accurately quote a range of standards and legislation and show understanding of the differences between legislation, standards and codes of practice.

The British Standards Institute

The **British Standards Institute (BSI)** works with industry, the British government and overseas standards authorities to produce a set of voluntary standards that state essential technical requirements or performance codes.

- The BSI can test products and award a certification to say that the product conforms to the stated British or European standard.
- The **BSI Kitemark** on a product is a quality mark to assure consumers that the product well produced, safe and fit for purpose.
- The standards relating to textiles include matters such as sizing, garment safety, and fabric testing methods.

Measures to ensure the safety of toys

Toys available for retail must comply with the provisions of the Toys (Safety) Regulations (2011) and European Standard BS EN 71.

Some of the hazards associated with textile toys include:

- Soft toys with loose pile fabric or hair that sheds easily presenting a choking hazard.
- Toys with small components or parts such as buttons that detach and that could cause a child to choke.
- Loose ribbons on toys and long neck ties on children's costumes.
- Toys and dressing-up clothes that are flammable.
- Toys with residual or unrestricted toxic chemical substances such as some dyestuffs and finishing chemicals that may be ingested.
- Toys intended for children under 36 months that do not meet hygiene and cleanliness requirements and may increase the risk of infection, sickness or contamination.

Lion Mark

The Lion Mark is a recognisable consumer symbol representing safety and quality. It verifies that members of the British Toy and Hobby Association (BTHA), who conform to Toys (Safety) Regulations (2011), BS EN 71 and their own code of practice, have made the toy.

Advice to consumers

When buying textile products, consumers should try to buy from reputable retailers. They should look for safety and quality symbols and always read and follow specific safety warnings or product maintenance advice contained on labels.

> **Key terms**
>
> **British Standards Institute (BSI):** a national organisation that devises agreed standard procedures for performing a wide range of tasks.
>
> **BSI Kitemark:** a quality mark to show that a product conforms to agreed standards.

Now test yourself   TESTED ☐

1 Explain the responsibilities of an employer under the Health and Safety at Work Act (1974).
2 What is the role of the Health and Safety Executive (HSE)?
3 What are the four stages in a risk assessment cycle?
4 List three different safety standards related to the design of children's clothes.
5 What three requirements must goods meet under the Consumer Rights Act?

1.10 Protecting design and intellectual property (A-level only)

Intellectual property (IP) refers to creations of the mind. It is a novel idea that is turned into a physical creation that did not exist before, such as a book, a film or a car design. Novel ideas can be protected with **intellectual property rights (IPR)**.

Some rights are automatically given when work is created, for example copyright; others have to be applied for and paid for, for example a patent. IP disputes are more easily resolved if a designer's work is properly protected.

> **Key terms**
>
> **Intellectual property (IP):** ideas, artistic work or physical creations that are entitled to protection for the originator in the form of copyright, design rights, patent, registered design or trademark.
>
> **Intellectual property rights (IPR):** the legal protection of IP.

Copyright and design rights

REVISED

Copyright legally protects the use of a designer's artwork, illustrations or photographs once it has been physically expressed.
- To copyright work, and assert ownership, the designer adds the © symbol, their name and the date to the work.
- Copyright law sets out the rights of the owner and manages the permissions to use copyrighted work, for example licences that can be drawn up for others to pay to use the work.
- The UK Copyright, Designs and Patents Act 1988 provides cover for most works for 70 years after the death of the creator.

Textile designs are automatically protected by the **design right** for 15 years after creation and for 10 years after it is first sold.
- It is not necessary to register the design right, but ownership is hard to prove if designs are unregistered.
- To register the design right, copies of early drafts, designs and design modifications are signed and dated by the designer and verified by a solicitor, who keeps them as proof of ownership.

> **Key term**
>
> **Copyright:** unregistered rights that protect original works such as books, plays, artwork, illustrations or photographs.
>
> **Design right:** gives automatic protection to the appearance of a product but provides only some legal protection for designers to stop unauthorised copying.

> **Typical mistake**
>
> Don't focus only on copyright; remember that there are lots of different IPRs designers can use to protect their designs and intellectual property.

Registered designs and patents

REVISED

Registered designs offer legal protection for a product's shape, appearance and decoration. Designs can be registered for up to 25 years by submitting illustrations and a fee to the **Intellectual Property Office (IPO)**.

A **patent** prevents others from manufacturing, using, selling or importing the new invention without the inventor's permission. To apply for a patent, inventors have to submit detailed labelled diagrams and clear descriptions to the IPO.
- Patents provide up to 20 years' legal protection but are expensive and complicated to obtain.
- In order to be awarded a patent, a new creation or invention needs to be useful and original.
- Patents are not meant for aesthetic, creative or artistic work.
- Patents apply only to the working parts of a design.

> **Key terms**
>
> **Registered design:** legal protection for a product's appearance or decoration to stop unauthorised copying.
>
> **Intellectual Property Office (IPO):** the official UK government body responsible for IP.
>
> **Patent:** legal protection for inventions relating to the way in which a product functions.

Trademarks and logos

A **trademark** is a recognisable and unique combination of words, sounds, colours and logos used to identify and promote a brand, product or organisation. A **logo** is a graphical symbol designed to be instantly identifiable and unique in order to stand out.

Trademarks and logos are commonly used in the textile industry to provide legal protection for a brand identity and to help with marketing.

- Trademarks need to be applied for and renewed every ten years.
- The IPO collects the fees and registers the trademarks.
- The ™ symbol shows that a product is yet to be registered.
- The ® symbol warns others that it is a protected trademark and makes it easier to take legal action against counterfeiters.
- An example is Burberry's dispute with Target over sales of fashion products using the iconic Burberry check trademark.

> ### Key terms
>
> **Trademark:** a unique combination of words, sounds, colours and logos used for marketing, and the legal protection of brand identity.
>
> **Logo:** an instantly identifiable graphic symbol or design used alongside a trademarked brand identity.

Now test yourself

TESTED

1 What is meant by the term 'intellectual property'?
2 What is the difference between copyright and design right?
3 List the three main intellectual property rights (IPR) used to protect designers.
4 Explain how one IPR is used to protect designers. Include at least one specific product example in your answer.
5 Draw the symbols used to denote copyright, a registered trademark and an unregistered trademark.

Figure 1.10.1 Counterfeit bags on sale in the street

Exam tip

When asked to explain how designers can protect their designs and intellectual property, include a wide range of IPR. Illustrate your answer with product or company examples and don't forget to demonstrate your knowledge by including positive as well as negative points relating to different IPR.

1.11 Design for manufacture, maintenance, disposal and repair

Reference should also be made to Chapters 1.2, 2.3, 2.8 and 2.9.

Manufacture, repair, maintenance and disposal

The textile industry is responsible for high levels of waste and pollution across the world. In addition, consumers are buying more and more low-cost garments, and are more likely to throw them away and buy new than to repair them. Most companies promote ethical practices – largely in respect of sourcing and manufacture – but disposal remains a significant global issue.

Reducing the number of manufacturing processes (A-level only)

Careful planning and management of each of the many stages and processes that are involved in making a textile product will not only save time and resources but will also minimise levels of waste and pollution.

These stages include processing the raw materials to make yarn or fabric, cutting and sewing products, and packaging and delivering products to the retailer.

Processing raw materials

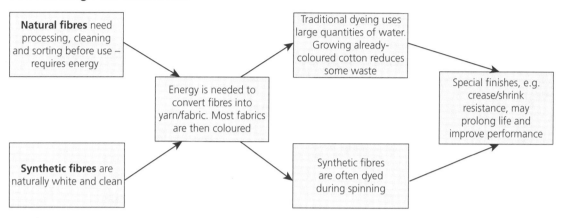

Figure 1.11.1 Processing raw materials

Cutting and sewing

The design and style of a product will dictate the cutting and sewing processes required. Managing the processes can lead to a reduction in the use of resources. For example:

- Choice of fabric – bias cut, one-way designs, naps will require more fabric.
- Using fewer seams – results in fewer seam allowances and therefore less fabric and thread being used. For example, a jacket could be made by cutting on a fold line, rather than using a centre back seam.
- Using fewer components – for example, reducing the number of buttons used, which also saves thread.
- Using computer-aided manufacture (CAM) – more accurate cutting creates less waste.

Packaging and delivery

Packaging is important in order to protect products while they are being batched for delivery so that they arrive at the retailers in perfect condition. However, reducing the amount of packing required saves on resources and reduces weight, which means reduced delivery costs.

Modern transport systems can reduce the need for packaging, for example transporting garments on moveable rails facilitates immediate display at the retailer and reduces the need to iron the garments to remove creases.

Reducing extravagant or unnecessary packaging also reduces the consumption of resources.

Figure 1.11.2 Some clothes come with excessive – and therefore unnecessary – packaging

Choice of materials

Careful consideration should be given to the choice of materials used in a product and this includes thinking about the consumer's requirements, its intended use, aftercare and disposal:

- The choice of fabrics and components depends on the required performance of a product, for example fabrics that need careful handling, such as chiffon and velvets, or fabrics that pill easily, will degrade more quickly in products that are worn and washed frequently.
- The application of finishes such as stain repellents or crease-resistant finishes can improve performance, making products last longer, and reduce the amount of washing and ironing required.
- The chemicals in laundry detergents, fabric softeners and dry-cleaning fluids damage the environment, for example by **eutrophication**. Choosing fabrics that are easier to clean can minimise this damage.
- Washing at high temperatures and ironing incur energy costs – using synthetic fabrics, for example, can lower these energy demands.
- Fabric mixtures can be difficult to recycle as the fibres can be difficult to separate. Using new environmentally friendly fibres, such as lyocell, can reduce the consumption of resources.
- Using biodegradable fibres rather than synthetic fibres can reduce the toxicity of landfill sites.

Advisory labelling (A-level only)

See Chapter 1.9 for more on advisory labelling.

The six Rs of sustainability

Responsible designing and manufacturing takes account of the six Rs of **sustainability**, as discussed below.

Reduce

Modifying the design of a product to reduce the amount of fabric and components used results in the saving of materials and energy used in manufacture. Designing products for longer life should also mean that fewer products are required.

Recycle

If textile products are recycled, there will be significant reduction in:
- the use of natural resources, for example water
- the need for chemicals in manufacture
- pollution caused by the manufacturing processes.

All products can be recycled in one way or another. They can be:
- resold to charity shops or sent abroad to developing countries for reuse
- broken down and restructured, for example to make insulating materials and paper
- used as products for different purposes, for example wiping cloths
- made from recycled, non-textile materials, for example plastic can be recycled into polyester to make fleece fabrics.

Reuse

Upcycling fabrics to make new products is an increasingly popular method of reusing textiles. H&M and Marks & Spencer have introduced garment collection boxes in their stores to encourage customers to donate unwanted clothing.

Rethink

Rethinking how products are made or used can improve sustainability. For example, the production, manufacture and care of polyester fibres

> **Key terms**
>
> **Eutrophication:** excessive richness of nutrients in a lake or other body of water caused by the phosphates found in laundry detergents as well as fertilisers used on plants. May result in oxygen depletion of the water.
>
> **Sustainability:** the reduction of all aspects of design and manufacturing activity that have a negative impact on the environment or the lives of humans.

> **Typical mistake**
>
> Check your facts. It is a common error to state that polyester fibres are unsustainable and that cotton is very sustainable. Make sure you are able to justify your statements with explanations.

actually requires less energy, land and water resources than some other fibres, such as cotton, and therefore has less impact on the environment.

Energy consumption can be reduced by selecting processing techniques that use less energy and by reducing the distance raw materials have to travel. This reduces fuel consumption and wear and tear on the road system.

Repair

Designing products that are easy to repair and encouraging a culture of repair makes garments more sustainable:

- Minor, timely repairs extend the life of a garment – 'a stitch in time', 'make do and mend'.
- Components, such as buttons, are easy to replace.
- Holes in well-worn areas can be covered with patches, for example jacket elbows. In some clothing, for example for young children, this can be included in the design.
- Holes in knitted fabrics can be darned.
- Services are often available at dry cleaners to replace broken zips or the linings in jackets and coats.

Refuse

Special offers and marketing campaigns encourage us to buy more clothes than is really necessary, but consumers can refuse to buy environmentally unsustainable products and reduced demand will lead to better practices. For example, consumers are now more reluctant to buy products made by workers exploited by factories that pay very low wages.

> **Exam tip**
>
> If you are explaining sustainability issues, don't forget the six Rs. Include specific examples for all six in your response.

Care and maintenance of products

REVISED

Keeping textile products in good condition prolongs their useful life. This involves being able to clean, repair and store them in a way that does not cause any damage.

The care labels found on textile products help consumers by providing washing, drying and ironing instructions as well as other relevant information about the fabric composition.

Table 1.11.1 Care instructions on labels

Care symbol	Standard instructions
Washing temperature	A tub with a number inside indicates the maximum washing temperature in °C.
	A tub with bars under it indicates the agitation required. Two bars mean much less agitation.
	A tub with a hand above means hand wash only.
	A tub with an X through it means do not wash.
Bleaching	An empty triangle means any kind of bleach can be used.
	A triangle with parallel diagonal lines in it means use a non-chlorine bleach.
	A triangle with an X through it means do not bleach.

Care symbol	Standard instructions
Drying	The drying symbol comes with lines in it: • A curved line means line dry. • A horizontal line means dry flat. • Three vertical lines mean drip dry. A circle within the square means tumble dry.
Ironing temperature	The ironing symbol comes with dots in it indicating the ironing temperature: • 1 dot = cool iron. • 2 dots = medium iron. • 3 dots = hot iron.
Dry cleaning	An empty circle means the product should be dry cleaned. The dry cleaning symbol can come with the letters P or F in it to indicate the solvent to be used in professional dry cleaning. The level of agitation required is indicated by bars under the circle. Two bars is very gentle cleaning. An X through the circle means do not dry clean.

Designers also need to consider other issues that can affect the care and maintenance of textile products:

- The effect of heat on thermoplastic fibres – washing or ironing at high temperatures can heat-set unwanted creases into the product.
- The fabric structure, any applied finishes and the garment construction that may need specific care, for example loosely knitted fabric, flame-resistant fabric or the use of linings, shoulder pads or trims.
- The type of detergents used, for example alkaline and enzyme-based detergents can have a detrimental effect on some fibres such as silk and wool.
- What happens during storage, for example protein fibres can be attacked by moths, white wool and polyamide turn yellow in UV light and mildew will affect damp cotton.

Now test yourself

TESTED

1 Woven fabrics are more stable than knitted fabrics. True or false. Explain your understanding of a stable fabric.
2 Explain your understanding of the potential hazards created by the use of laundry detergents.
3 What resources, other than water, are conserved when recycling textile products?
4 Lyocell is a more sustainable fibre than cotton. Name another three fibres that are more sustainable.
5 What are the main natural resources required in the production of cotton?

1.12 Feasibility studies (A-level only)

Producing and testing prototypes

REVISED

To check if a design proposal will be effective in meeting the needs of the target market, the development team will carry out a feasibility study.

They will test the **prototype**, gather feedback from the target market and evaluate the need for any required changes. The design may be developed further as a result and new prototypes may be made.

Feedback from the target market can be sought by conducting one-to-one interviews or **focus groups** (see Chapter 2.1. page 100). Questions can be asked about:

- the performance of the product
- the ease and comfort of using it
- the ease of cleaning or maintaining it
- whether its features are suitable, for example pockets/fastenings
- the cost
- any recommended improvements.

Such questions should result in constructive feedback about possible modifications, for example improved performance or target market appeal.

Key terms

Prototype: the first version of a design to see it if works as intended, and to find out if improvements are necessary.

Focus group: a panel of consumers who rate the product and feed back their opinions. Those taking part will be from the target group.

Analysing consumer feedback

Market research will collect data about potential buyers and their preferences, for example preferred colours, length or shape. The statistical data can then be analysed using pie charts, graphs and histograms. The results are used to evaluate the design.

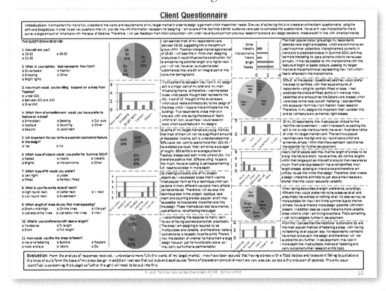

Figure 1.12.1 Student example of questionnaire analysis using charts and graphs

Product scale and dimensions

REVISED

Feasibility studies also consider the effect of the product style on the cost of materials as this will affect the product's retail cost. For example, longer dress lengths will require more fabric.

Where the product is to be sold is another consideration, as standard sizes differ across the world and garments need to be sized appropriately. Designers and product developers are guided by the use of **anthropometric** data (see Chapter 1.8, page 69), and a **pattern grader** will adjust pattern proportions to give a range of different sizes for the same product.

Key terms

Anthropometrics: scientific measurements of the human body applied to the design of products.

Pattern grading: pattern designers use anthropometric and ergonomic data to grade patterns for different sizes.

Table 1.12.1 Different standard sizes for the same product

Country	Standard size
United Kingdom	10
United States	8
Japan	9–11
France, Spain and Portugal	38
Germany and Scandinavia	36
Italy	42
Australia and New Zealand	10

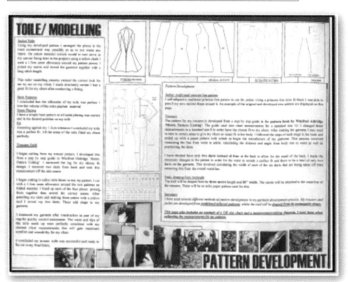

Figure 1.12.2 Student example of pattern development using anthropometrics

Now test yourself

TESTED

1 Explain your understanding of the work of a pattern grader.
2 Explain how a prototype plays a major role in the iterative design process.
3 Why do feasibility studies play an important role in the textile industry?

1.13 Enterprise and marketing in the development of products

Enterprise and marketing

REVISED

Enterprises

An enterprise is a business that sells products or services to make a profit. It is usually set up by an **entrepreneur** who has created a new idea or identified an opportunity in the market and takes the risk of putting it into practice.

Fashion and textiles enterprises could include:

- new start-ups
- online businesses
- project businesses, for example launched by a celebrity
- community projects, for example recycling enterprises

Key term

Entrepreneur: a person who demonstrates initiative and invests capital into an idea by setting up a business, project or other venture.

Marketing

Marketing is developing a product so that it appeals to the target market:

- Products need to be at the right price and readily available.
- Products need to be advertised to create demand.
- Shoppers need to be made aware of new products.
- Sales data need to be analysed as part of market research to direct product development.

Advertising and promotion are focused on the most likely target market through the use of:

- website promotions and advice
- social media, such as Facebook and Instagram
- online vlogs (video blogs) demonstrating the product
- online pop-up adverts
- promotional events
- media adverts (in newspapers and on television and radio)
- shop-front displays
- packaging
- display boards.

Brand identity

Brand identity is the way in which a business presents itself to, and wants to be perceived by, its consumers. A short, easily remembered phrase or strapline is often used by organisations or retailers to communicate their brand identity.

Customer identification

An essential element of successful marketing is being able to identify a customer's age, gender, location and lifestyle. Such data are used to build a client profile through which product requirements can be developed and marketing campaigns can be more effectively targeted.

Customer Identity and Access Management (CIAM) is a system used by companies to securely acquire and handle such customer data.

Figure 1.13.1 Student example of a client profile

Labelling

Product labels, including fabric labels, embroidered logos and swing tickets identify and promote the product brand.

> **Exam tip**
>
> If you are answering a question about marketing a product, identify different channels of communication and explain why they are effective. Use specific examples of companies and products.

> **Key term**
>
> **Brand identity:** the distinctive and memorable style, ethos and values of a business.

Packaging

Packaging protects the product so that the customer receives it in good condition, but it can also be used to promote the brand and build brand loyalty.

Corporate identity

The aim of establishing a **corporate identity** is to make sure that employees and customers understand the company's trading principles. It is usually expressed visually through the use of:

- logos and trademarks
- shop signage
- shop/outlet design
- staff uniforms
- company stationery and packaging.

> **Key term**
>
> **Corporate identity:** the visual representation of the business, for example through the use of logos and trademarks.

Global marketing (A-level only)

Global marketing is where a company adapts its marketing strategies in order to sell products internationally. The marketing of fashion products globally has been affected by:

- the demand from culturally diverse countries for western fashion
- rising affluence in emerging countries, for example India, increasing demand
- the rise of new, talented designers worldwide being publicised.

Social media and viral marketing play a key part in any global marketing strategy. By using social media to promote products, companies can:

- reach a global market immediately
- target customers relatively cheaply compared to traditional advertising
- network and build up a community of potential customers, for example through Facebook, Twitter and Instagram.

Product costing and profit

To compete and appeal to the target market, products have to be realistically priced. However, in order to conduct their business, retailers also need to make a profit. Balancing the costs of making the product with the final selling price is part of the product development process, and manufacturers and suppliers will consult with fashion buyers regarding potential new ranges.

> **Typical mistake**
>
> Be specific about the different aspects of marketing that create brand identity and give examples, for example the advantages of client profiles, the need for corporate identity, the role labels and packaging play.

The role of entrepreneurs

Entrepreneurs are people who look for new business opportunities. They come up with new, creative ideas and take the risk of putting their ideas into practice. Entrepreneurs typically network and collaborate with others to develop their ideas. In so doing, they often inspire and mentor others, and have links with charities and educational bodies.

Collaborative working

Increasingly, brands, designers and other creative people will work together in partnerships or collectives to develop new and innovative fashion, clothing and textile products.

This is effective for the generation of creative ideas, as skills can be combined, and support and encouragement can be given for creativity and innovation. It also helps to expand a customer base and reduce business costs as workspace, facilities and specialist equipment can be shared.

Factors affecting product price (A-level only)

The product price must reflect the costs of making and distributing the product, the business overheads and the profit required for the business. The price will also be determined by taking into account:

- the demand for the product
- the price of rival products
- the price per unit
- the potential for unsold stock
- the costs incurred by online sales versus retail properties
- the recommended retail price (RRP), which allows retailers enough money to pay their business running costs and earn a profit.

Table 1.13.1 Factors affecting product price

Costs	Includes the costs of materials and components and takes into account overheads, for example marketing, administration, packaging and transport.
Profit margin	The amount of money gained from selling products after all costs have been deducted, expressed as a percentage. A low profit margin means that costs are too high or the price is too low.
Target market	A particular group of people defined by factors such as age, gender, interests, location, disposable income at which a product or service is aimed.
Budget	A realistic calculation of the income required to fund a complete project.

Fashion cycles (A-level only)

REVISED

In a **fashion cycle**, a new fashion is sported by trendsetters, the fashion becomes popular, its popularity reaches a peak, the fashion then declines and disappears.

Sales and marketing cycles

The sales and marketing cycle is the sequence of advertising and promotional events that attracts customers, communicates with them and persuades them to buy the product.

Different marketing strategies are used according whether the product is:
- a fad – a short-lived craze
- a classic – a simple, elegant design that stays in fashion
- a standard – a popular style that lasts longer than a fad but shorter than a classic.

The impact of fashion on trends

Commercial fashion is often influenced by extreme fashions from non-mainstream groups, for example punk. Other influential trends include:
- **Retro:** sometimes referred to as 'vintage inspired', these fashions are retrospective in that they are derived from past fashions and designs.
- **Vintage:** the use of actual items from the past. This fashion shows an appreciation of colours, patterns and fabrics from the past, for example the Art Deco period.
- **Industrial:** black or military-influenced clothing, which emerged in the late 1980s. It is often associated with anti-establishment, sci-fi or post-apocalyptic themes, for example steampunk.
- **Traditional:** a trend inspired by traditional styles and fabrics, for example Harris tweed hacking jackets and tartan kilts.

> **Key term**
>
> **Fashion cycle:** how a fashion trend begins, becomes popular, becomes unfashionable, then disappears.

Figure 1.13.2 1955 fashion photograph of a classic cardigan

Industry development cycles

The traditional fashion seasons are spring/summer and autumn/winter, and the average lead time to develop a collection for each season is 18–24 months. However, mid-season ranges and mini-collections play an increasing part as fast changes in the industry encourage consumers to look for new designs.

Colour trends

Fashion colours change from season to season and designers and manufacturers need to make sure their products will be on trend to be successful. Fashion forecasting is a global industry, with **trend forecasters** such as World Global Style Network (WGSN) producing reports that forecast future style themes, colours, fibres and directions. Forecasted colour charts can be supplied to help designers plan their collections.

Fibre trends

The latest developments in fibres are incorporated into new fabric ranges to offer improved aesthetics and performance, for example easy care/stain-resistant fabrics.

The use of environmentally friendly fibres has been a growing trend, for example fibres made from recycled polyester, or fibres such as lyocell, hemp and bamboo that are grown sustainably.

Predictions

Manufacturers and suppliers need to ensure their products will be popular and successful to stay in business. Trend predictions provide catwalk analysis and summaries of up-to-date fashion directions that will help businesses to plan ahead with knowledge and confidence.

Trade fairs

Fashion trade fairs such as Premiere Vision in Paris showcase the latest trends in materials (fabrics, trimmings, buttons, fastenings) and also technological developments. They keep in line with the industry development cycles of 18–24 months and show twice a year to fashion designers and product developers. They provide an opportunity to get new ideas, network with others, and source and buy materials.

The influence of trends and changes in lifestyles

The style of clothing and textile products is influenced by trends and changes in lifestyle. For example:
- **Work:** this has become less formal, leading to 'dress down' days and a demand for more comfortable work clothing.
- **Health and fitness:** this has become a popular leisure pursuit, leading to a demand for fashionable leisure wear.
- **New technologies:** the use of devices such as smartphones, tablets and computers have led to design modifications in bags, hats and jackets to accommodate them.
- **The cult of the individual:** people are free to develop their own personal style and dress eclectically, leading to a demand for more customised products.
- **Internet access/social media:** allows fashion trends to be communicated very quickly.
- **Travel opportunities:** as more people travel more frequently, holiday clothing needs to be available all year round.

Figure 1.13.3 Industrial-style clothing

Figure 1.13.4 Traditional-style clothing

Key term

Trend forecasts: predictions for future fashions produced by forecasting businesses and sold to fashion design companies.

Figure 1.13.5 New technology included in bag design

1   What is your understanding of a start-up enterprise within the fashion/textile industry?
2   Explain how modern technology can assist in the collection of data to make a customer profile.
3   What information can usually be found on a product label?
4   Identify the advantages to designers of working collaboratively.
5   Outline the history of the sports bra to understand the resurgence of this garment.
6   Explain your understanding of the fashion influences that inspired the industrial trend.

1.14 Design communication

A range of methods and techniques can be used to communicate information about design proposals:

- Visual methods: mood boards, photographs, technical drawings.
- Written methods: reports, summaries, evaluations, annotations.
- Numerical methods: charts, graphs, tables.

Some presentations will combine these methods, for example manufacturing specifications might include information in the form of technical drawings, annotations and numerical tables.

The example student mood board shown in Figure 1.14.1 communicates the colours evocative of the design theme, the environmental issues that have been considered and the possible fabric effects that could be used.

Figure 1.14.1 Example student mood board

Report writing

REVISED

Written reports are formal documents that contain detailed information about proposed designs. They are shared with co-workers and clients so consideration must be given to the readers of the report. The content should be presented in a standard format and be easily understood.

Table 1.14.1 What items to include in a formal report

Item	Content
Brief summary/**abstract**	A summary of the design project
Short introduction	An explanation of the context for the design task and the objectives of the project
References	A list of the research activities undertaken to investigate the design brief
Explanations	Explanations of how ideas were tested and developed
Prototype	A description of the prototype and its main features
Relevant issues	Notes about any safety issues or hazards associated with the design and manufacture of the product
Associated costs	Notes about the costs associated with the design, and possible modifications
Environmental impact	Notes about the environmental impact of sourcing materials and methods of production, and possible modifications
Manufacturability	Notes about the manufacturability of the design, and possible modifications or improvements
Summary of results	The results of testing the final design against the design criteria, prototype trials, customer feedback
Conclusions	An analysis of the strengths and weaknesses of the design and suggested improvements
Appendix	Further details about any of the data mentioned in the report
Bibliography	References to sources of information used in the writing of the report

Key term

Abstract: a brief summary of the report, which helps the reader quickly grasp the content.

Graphs, tables and charts

REVISED

Graphs

Graphs are used to present numerical data in a visual way that can be quickly understood. They can show how data change over time. The unit of measurement is plotted on the y-axis on the left-hand side, and the timeline is given on the x-axis at the bottom of the graph. For example, line graphs can be used to show buying patterns over a period of time, which is helpful for stock control on the shop floor.

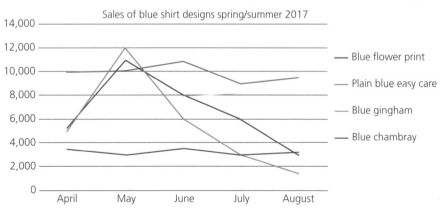

Figure 1.14.2 Line graph to show sales of blue shirt designs over a five-month period

Tables and charts

Tables organise data in a clear and structured way, allowing you to interpret the data and identify patterns or missing data.

The student example in Figure 1.14.3 shows how a table has been used to clearly record each point of their research analysis. Images of research pages have also been included to enhance the communication of the data.

Figure 1.14.3 Student research analysis

Charts are a visual representation of factual/statistical data collected through research and testing. They are used to make large quantities of data easier to read.

Some types of chart are more useful for certain purposes, for example pie charts are useful for displaying percentages. Selecting the most appropriate chart to display the data will make the presentation more effective. Examples are given below, displaying data about the colours of boys' T-shirts.

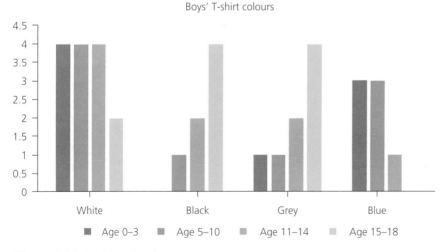

Figure 1.14.4 A bar chart

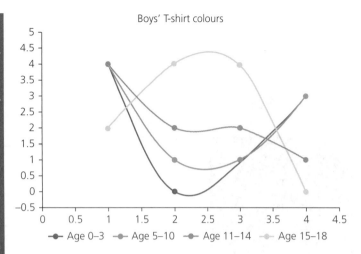

Figure 1.14.6 **A scatter diagram**

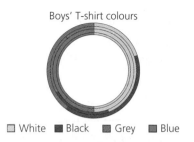

Figure 1.14.5 **A donut chart**

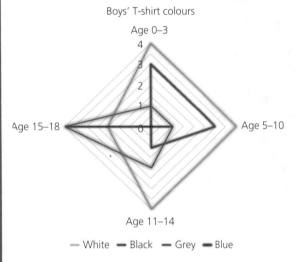

Figure 1.14.7 **A radar chart**

Histograms are used to show distributions of variables and present quantitative data. They look similar to bar charts but bar charts are used to compare variables and show categorical data.

More than one method of displaying results in a visual format can be used, for example different aspects of research findings can be analysed by using bar charts and/or pie charts.

Typical mistake

Make sure you include all of your workings out in questions involving mathematical calculations. You might arrive at the wrong final answer but your method of calculation may still gain you some marks.

Key terms

Radar chart: a chart with a central point and radiating arms to display multiple sets of data on a single chart. Also known as a spider chart.

Histogram: a chart with bars used to show the distribution of numerical data.

Exam tip

Make sure you are familiar with the use and value of statistical information through the design development process. Be able to explain the advantages of selecting different methods of presenting data that will be collected through evaluations, for example quantitative and qualitative data.

2D/3D sketching

REVISED

Quick, 2D sketches are usually used by designers to communicate their initial ideas to other members of the design team, and to those involved in the development, costing and production of the product.

3D sketching is then used to add more detail, develop the concept further and make the ideas more concrete. 3D sketching would elaborate on details such as the shape, style, pattern, colour and texture of the product. The developed design will provide a shared vision for the whole design team.

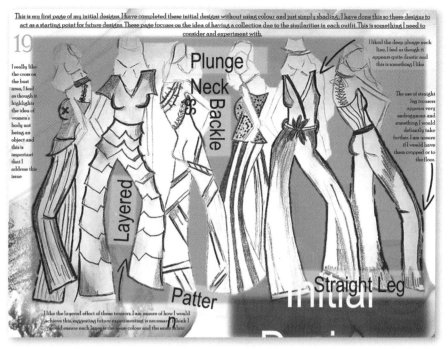

Figure 1.14.8 Student example of a quick sketch

Figure 1.14.9 Student example of a sketch for a more developed design

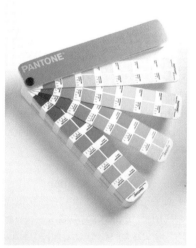

Figure 1.14.10 Pantone colour chart

Designers can communicate the particular colours they want by using the Pantone colour-matching system. This recognised system of classifying colours provides clear and universally understood reference points in order to select the exact colour.

Use of mixed media and rendering to enhance drawings

Drawings can be created in a variety of ways:
- Base: any surface suitable for sketching, drawing or collage can be used, for example all types of paper and card.
- Medium: graphite, coloured pencil, chalk, charcoal, crayon, ink, ballpoint, paint can all be used.

- Mixed media: a combination, for example of painted paper or magazine pages used for collage, and textures created by wax resist with water colour.
- **Rendering**: the process of adding colour, shading and texture to an image, which can be used to create 3D effects.

The student example in Figure 1.14.11 shows how mixed media and rendering has been used to successfully create an impact on a presentation board.

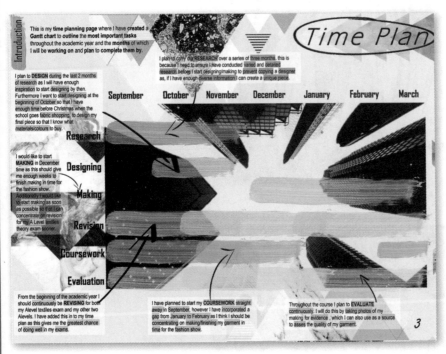

Figure 1.14.11 Student presentation board

Dimensioning and details for manufacture   REVISED

Working drawings

Often referred to as 'fashion flats' or 'flats', working drawings are precise, technical drawings that communicate the dimensions of the product to the manufacturer. They will include:

- the front and back view
- the design features
- accurate measurements
- the position of pockets, buttons, zips
- close-ups to show fine detail
- details of stitching and trims.

Geometry

Geometry is the field of mathematics concerned with shapes and their properties. It is an aspect of fashion design used for aesthetic appeal, for example gored skirts, V-necklines, asymmetrical hems, geometrical prints.

In the context of manufacture, geometry is used in technical specifications to achieve accuracy and to structure clothes, transforming 2D templates into 3D products, for example using darts.

SPECIFICATION SHEET

STYLE NO:
DESCRIPTION: LADIES' REVERSIBLE JACKET
DATE:

CUSTOMER:
CUST.#:
CUST. P/O

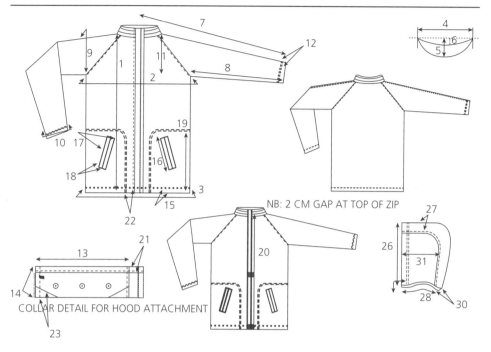

NB: 2 CM GAP AT TOP OF ZIP

COLLAR DETAIL FOR HOOD ATTACHMENT

Figure 1.14.12 Technical specification sheet created on Adobe Illustrator

In the student examples in Figures 1.14.13 and 1.14.14, a design has been tested and developed using geometric calculations. The final design and pattern development show the process with the use of 2D templates and a laser cutter.

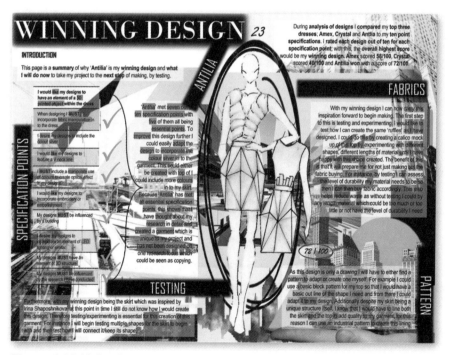

Figure 1.14.13 Student design using geometric calculations

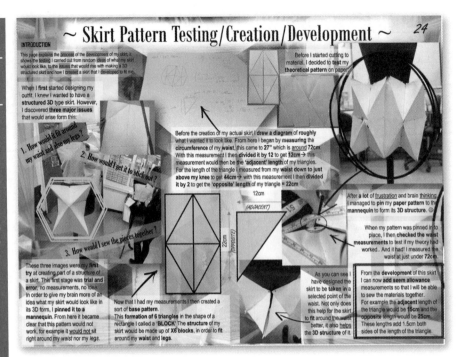

Figure 1.14.14 Student final design and pattern development

Now test yourself

1 Suggest ways in which different presentation strategies can combine efficiently to communicate an evaluation of a design proposal.
2 Explain how using charts as a method of presenting data can provide a clear analysis of research results.
3 What are the advantages of using the Pantone colour-matching system? Give examples.
4 Explain the details that should be included in a working drawing. Are there any advantages to the details being largely visual and numerical?

Exam practice

1 Describe two different fabric finishes that could be applied to polyester and viscose blended fabric to improve its performance.
2 Describe a weft knitted structure. You may use a diagram.
3 Describe the structure and properties of a staple yarn.
4 Name two fancy yarns.
5 Describe two ways in which smooth synthetic fibre filaments can be made into textured yarn.
6 Yarns that contain elastane fibres are usually core spun. Explain why these yarns need to be core spun.
7 Place each fibre listed below in the correct column of the table. You should use each fibre once only.
   Nylon   Bamboo   Mohair   Cotton   Tencel   Elastane   Acetate

Natural cellulose	Natural protein	Regenerated	Synthetic

8 The photograph shows a cushion for use on a kitchen or dining room chair. The fabric used will have been tested to ensure that it is durable enough to stand up to the expected wear and tear. Describe a test that the fabric technologist might have carried out to check the durability of the fabric.

9 Name two resist methods of applying colour to fabric.
10 The production and distribution of fashion products involves the use of automated machinery. Describe how computer-aided manufacture (CAM) is used for a range of different processes in the fashion industry.

ONLINE

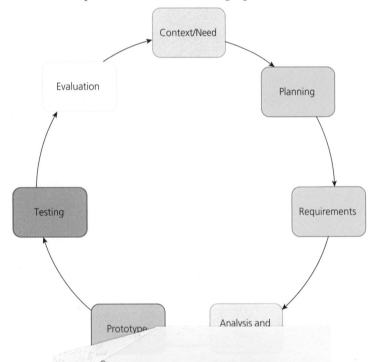

Part 2 Designing and making principles

2.1 Design *[processes]*

Iterative des*[ign]*

Fashion and textile des*[igners work]*
individually or in teams. Th*[...]*
on an efficient design process.

The **iterative design** process involves c*[ontinually testing]* and
refining a product as required to optimise the *[design.]*

- Iterative design is a cyclical process of designing *[– it is not a]* linear
  process.
- At each stage of design development, work is tested and evaluated.
- Designs may be trialled and modified several times before the
  prototype is finalised.

See also Chapter 2.4 for more on design processes.

> **Key term**
>
> **Iterative design:** a cyclical
> approach to the design and
> development process.

[Handwritten note:] Iterative design process. a cycle of sampling, testing, analysing and refining a design until the final design is created

Context/Need

Planning

Requirements

Analysis and

Prototype

Testing

Evaluation

Figure *[...]*

User-c*[entred design (UCD)]* is a design process focused around the needs
of the e*[nd user.]*
- dev*[...]*
- ider*[...]* when and why they will
  use
- inv*[...]*
- test

User-c*[...]* of views to find
out the *[...]*ve feedback from
potenti*[...]*

[Handwritten note:] User-centred design UCD developing new product according to what the consumer need or want. sometimes referred to as user driven development.

> **Key term**
>
> **User-centred design (UCD):**
> developing a new product to
> suit the needs and wants of
> the consumer.

Now te*[st yourself ...]*o.uk/myrevisionnotes

Designing to meet a need

A design solution often comes about because of a need or a demand for a new product. This might be driven by:

- a gap in the market, for example due to radical changes in men's fashion
- technological advances, for example wearable technology and clothing for extreme sports
- a desire for something original, for example bespoke designer products or catwalk garments that can be modified to meet individual needs.

Investigations to inform the use of primary and secondary data

Primary data

Primary data is new information gathered using direct research methods, including:

- consumer questionnaires and surveys
- telephone, online or face-to-face interviews
- focus groups
- customer panels
- product analysis.

The purpose of the research and its intended outcome must be clear as the results of these investigations will help to justify decisions made later in the design development process.

Secondary data

Secondary data is information that has previously been gathered by other researchers or businesses. Some may be gathered freely online or from printed resources, or it may be purchased from market research companies. It is important to remember that some secondary data could be out of date.

Sources of secondary data include:

- trend forecasts
- sales and company reports
- book research on styles or designer influences
- government publications
- media sources such as magazines and newspapers
- internet research
- trade association publications.

Market research

Market research involves the collection of data to establish if there is a need for a specific product. It will consider the target market, competitors and current trends. There are two types of market research data:

1 **Quantitative data**, which is factual, measurable information. Consumers answer yes/no questions or use tick boxes to state their preferences. Often in numerical form, such data can be categorised and analysed.
2 **Qualitative data**, which is subjective information and includes consumers' opinions and preferences or observations about their behaviour. Consumers give descriptive answers to questions to explain their point of view.

> **Typical mistake**
>
> Don't write in general terms. If you are writing about the design process and designing to meet a need, be specific and give an example, such as products being designed and modified due to advances in surface decoration, for example fabric printing techniques.

> **Key terms**
>
> **Primary data:** research carried out to collect new information.
>
> **Secondary data:** research collected from existing sources of data.

Interviews, either face to face or over the telephone are often used in market research. They provide insights into the needs and wants of the target market, and the information gathered can be either quantitative and qualitative data or both.

Human factors

For a design to function efficiently for people, anthropometric and ergonomic data must be taken into account. This will establish the correct size for the intended user and whether the product is fit for purpose.

Focus groups and customer panels

Focus groups are set up by market researchers to find out the views of the target market.

- A small group of between 6 and 10 people from the target market take part in a planned discussion about the product.
- There should be a good spread of the **demographic** within this group to provide a variety of opinions, for example age and gender.
- The feedback from the discussion is analysed and evaluated.
- Focus groups that meet regularly throughout product development are referred to as **customer panels**.

Product analysis and evaluation

Researchers and designers investigate existing, comparable products within the market to identify useful features. The data collected help them to develop ideas for new or improved products.

See Chapter 1.8, page 67 for more on product analysis.

Anthropometric data and percentiles

Anthropometric data tables provide standard measurements of the average human body. Designers and product developers use these data to make decisions about which sizes are appropriate for their target market. Pattern graders and manufacturers use the data to ensure uniformity in sizing.

Designers should make it clear whether the product is being designed for the average or the extremes of the target market. **Percentiles** are used to ensure a product can be used by the majority of the target market.

Ergonomi[c]

Ergonomics [...] products interact. Data are collected [...] during movement, f[...] have an impact on th[...] how much stretch is nee[...]red.

Anthropome[tric...] **grading**, where the pa[...] different sizes for the s[...]

Developm[ent]

In fashion de[...] tely new design or an[...]elopment of a design prop[...]

(handwritten notes overlaying text:) how people and products interact. — data collected from studies on human bodies – walking sitting — impact on shape and movement of garment

Key terms

Focus group: a panel of consumers who rate the product and feed back their opinions. Those taking part will be from the target group.

Demographics: a study of population statistics, for example age, gender, marital status, income and occupation.

Customer panels: a group of prospective customers who are frequently consulted on their opinions about a new product during the different stages of development.

Percentiles: a specific statistical percentage range, often used to define appropriate anthropometric data for design purposes.

Pattern grading: pattern designers use anthropometric and ergonomic data to grade patterns for different sizes.

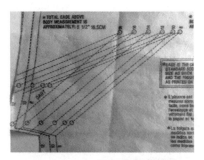

Figure 2.1.2 Commercial pattern with pattern grading for sizes 8 to 18

Planning and manufacture of a prototype solution

A sample machinist will make up the final prototype in exactly the same way as anticipated for the final manufacture. A detailed plan of prototype manufacture is drawn up, taking into account:
- the materials, techniques and processes to be used
- the tools and equipment required
- the QA procedures to be adopted
- the QC checks required during manufacture.

Planning the manufacture is an important step in ensuring that quality standards can be met in the final production.

The final prototype is tested and evaluated, with the involvement of the customer panel. This process will expose any necessary or desired modifications to make the manufacturing process cost effective.

Evaluation of a prototype solution to inform further development

The implementation of the iterative design process identifies and enables further modifications and improvements as the design process continues. Each round of testing and evaluation will involve further primary and secondary research to investigate other possible or suitable processes and techniques.

> **Exam tip**
>
> Read through the whole question before starting to answer so that relevant material can be included in each part of your answer. For example, if you are asked about the advantages of an iterative design process, explain the main principles of UCD. Apply your understanding in context, for example the designing of a uniform such as a corporate outfit for an airline. If possible, use annotated diagrams to illustrate your answer, for example a diagram showing the cyclical nature of the iterative design process.

Now test yourself

TESTED ☐

1 Explain your understanding of the iterative design process.
2 What is the difference between quantitative data and qualitative data?

2.2 Design theory

Design influences

REVISED ☐

Historical design styles, design movements and influential designers all have an influence on fashion and textile design and manufacture. Changes in fashion design have come about due to:
- social and cultural changes
- new technological advances
- economic and political developments
- the influence of the two world wars
- changing attitudes towards women's role in society
- austere and prosperous periods in history.

For more on the influence of designers, see Chapter 2.4.

Figure 2.2.1 Alexander McQueen's nature-inspired design

Design styles and movements

REVISED ☐

Table 2.2.1 Art Nouveau

Art Nouveau (1890–1910)	
Key points	A decorative art form influenced by organic shapes and structures popular in Europe and the United States.
Influences	A reaction to the academic art of the 19th century.
	Had similar ideals to the Arts and Crafts movement, which mourned the loss of hand-crafted skills.

> **Key term**
>
> **Art Nouveau:** an international style of decorative art, architecture and applied art inspired by organic shapes and structures.

→

Art Nouveau (1890–1910)	
Influences	However, Art Nouveau designs were more stylised and suitable for mass production.
	Liberty of London popularised Art Nouveau through its printed fabric designs, which featured organic flower shapes. In Italy, Art Nouveau was known as 'Stile Liberty'.
Features	Flowing dresses.
	Stylised flowers, leaves, roots, buds and seedpods.
	Curves.
	Ornate, nature-inspired designs featuring insect wings, feathers and vines.
Designers	Liberty (fabric prints), Charles Rennie Mackintosh (textile designs), Margaret MacDonald (embroidery and textiles), Alphonse Mucha (poster designs), Aubrey Beardsley (drawings), Louis Comfort Tiffany (lighting), René Lalique (glassware), Gustav Klimt (paintings), Antoni Gaudi (architecture), Hector Guimard (Paris Metro entrances).

Figure 2.2.2 Art Nouveau

Table 2.2.2 Art Deco

Art Deco (1920s and 1930s)	
Key points	Design work influenced by contemporary modern art. The style relied on bold designs that used clear, sleek lines, vibrant colours and geometric shapes and patterns. Reflected the machine age of cars, trains and ocean liners.
	Art Deco began in Europe, particularly Paris, in the early 20th century, but didn't really take hold until after the First World War. Its dominance ended with the Second World War.
Influences	The International Exhibition of Modern and Decorative and Industrial Arts in Paris in 1925.
	The modern geometric designs of cars, trains, automobiles and skyscrapers of the era.
	Jazz music.
	The bright colours of the **Fauvism** art movement and the costumes for Diaghilev's Ballet Russes.
	The exotic styles of China, Japan, India, Persia and ancient Egypt.
Features	High-end fashion featured materials such as silk and beaded velvet fabrics.
	Cloche hats and shorter hair styles ('the bob'), shorter hemlines, practical styles.
	Women started wearing trousers.
	Less curvy silhouettes and a flattening of the chest to give a more boyish look (**the garçonne look**).
	The flapper dress: a tubular dress with pleats, gathers or slits at the knees to allow greater movement.
	By the 1930s, the Art Deco style had begun to take on a softer look, with curved lines.

Key terms

Art Deco: a style of visual arts, architecture and design that first appeared in France before the First World War featuring modern geometric designs.

Fauvism: a style of art that emphasised the use of strong colour over representation or realistic values.

The garçonne look: a slim style of clothes giving a boyish silhouette, popular in the 1920s.

Figure 2.2.3 Art Deco-style evening dress

Art Deco (1920s and 1930s)	
Designers	Sonia Delaunay (textile and costume designs), Henri Matisse (paintings), Romain de Tirtoff, also known as Erté (costume designs), Frank Lloyd Wright (architecture), René Lalique (glassware), Clarisse Cliff (ceramics).

Table 2.2.3 Pop Art

Pop Art (1950s and 1960s)	
Key points	Bold, bright colours taken from everyday images seen in popular culture, for example food packaging, comics, adverts, pop music and Hollywood films.
Influences	A challenge to fine art ideals after the Second World War. The creation of art for a young audience. The democratisation of fashion. Mass-produced fashion that appealed to the consumer society, providing affordable fashion for the youth market. Andy Warhol and his Campbell's disposable 'Souper Dress' became a recognisable and popular design. Yves Saint Laurent's Pop Art collection of 1966.
Features	Bold bright, primary colours, repeating patterns, often shiny synthetic fabrics, for example shiny, wet-look PVC, easy-care acrylics and polyesters. Pop Art continues to be the most referenced art movement in fashion. Even today, manufacturers are incorporating sketches from Roy Lichtenstein in their trainers and footwear.
Designers	Artists including Andy Warhol, Roy Lichtenstein, Takashi Murakami, Keith Haring, Yayoi Kusama.

Typical mistake

Don't confuse Art Nouveau with Art Deco. There are some strong similarities between the two movements but the design influences are completely different. Art Nouveau is organic, Art Deco is more geometric.

Key term

Pop Art: an art movement inspired by popular culture that emerged in Britain and America in the mid to late 1950s.

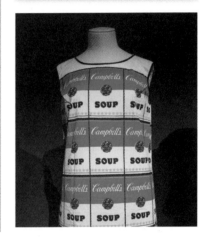

Figure 2.2.4 The Souper Dress

Table 2.2.4 Minimalism

Minimalism (1950s–1970s)	
Key points	Gender-neutral and functional designs. The main concept of minimalism is to strip everything down to its essential quality and achieve simplicity.
Influences	In times of austerity it is seen as an antidote to excess and complexity of colour, pattern and ornamentation. The reactions against feminism in the 1950s and 1980s saw a return of the hyper-feminine look, for example Dior's New Look, which was again overturned by experimental designers guided by minimalism.
Features	Concentrates more on the form and fabric than on the function of the clothing, strips the design object to its necessary elements. Designers are most likely to work with lines and geometric and sculptural shapes in a monochrome palette. Uses new technology and modern materials, fastenings are subtle and inconspicuous. Little ornamentation.
Designers	Artists including Donald Judd, John McCracken, Agnes Martin. Fashion designers including Shilpa Shah, Karla Gallardo, Diana Zwetzich, Halston, Calvin Klein, Helmut Lang, Courréges.

Table 2.2.5 Punk

Punk (mid-1970s onwards)	
Key points	Anti-establishment, seditionist and political. Androgynous in appearance, deliberately offensive. Defiantly anti-materialistic.
Influences	Punk rock music popular with demoralised and unemployed youngsters. Punk musicians were anti-establishment in both their lyrics and appearance. Punk clothing, which was initially handmade, became mass-produced by the 1980s and was sold in record stores and in some smaller speciality clothing stores. In the United Kingdom, 1970s punk fashion influenced the designs of Vivienne Westwood and Malcolm McLaren.
Features	Deliberately offensive T-shirts were popular in the early punk scene. Leather jackets, customised blazers and dress shirts were randomly covered in slogans, 'blood', patches and controversial images. T-shirts, like other punk clothing items, were often torn on purpose. Punk was deliberately ugly. Black became a prime fashion colour. Tapered jeans, tight leather pants, trousers with leopard patterns and bondage pants were popular choices.
Designers	Fashion designers including Vivienne Westwood, Anna Sui, Jean Paul Gaultier, Zandra Rhodes, Kawakubo, Charles Jeffrey.

Exam tip

Wherever possible use sketches to illustrate your understanding of styles from a particular era but make sure they are relevant/specific to the question. Well-annotated diagrams will help you achieve higher marks.

Figure 2.2.5 Punk

Designers and their work

REVISED

You need to understand some of the influences of a range of fashion designers and be aware of examples of their work.

Table 2.2.6 Paul Poiret (A-level only)

Paul Poiret (1879–1944)	
French fashion designer and master couturier.	
Designer information	**Design work**
Most prolific in his design work between 1900–1920.	Famous for his contentious kimono coat.
Major contribution was his use of **draping**.	Designed loose-fitting designs that freed women from restrictive underwear.
Renowned for his use of bright colours and exotic embellishments.	**Harem pantaloons**.
Pioneered the use of photography – the modern technology of the time – for fashion marketing.	Lampshade tunics featured in his fashion shoots.
Transformed the spirit of Art Deco into avant-garde garments.	Oriental-style turban hats.

Key terms

Draping: the process of arranging and pinning fabric on a mannequin to develop the shape of a garment. After arranging, the fabric is removed and used to create the pattern for construction.

Harem pantaloons: a Turkish-style trouser with narrow ankles introduced into western fashion by Paul Poiret in about 1910.

Table 2.2.7 Coco Chanel

Coco Chanel (1883–1971)	
French fashion designer and business woman who first became successful in 1915 during the First World War.	
Designer information	**Design work**
Moved away from corseted styles.	Designs were more informal and elegantly sporty.
Designed for more active lifestyles, which meant clothing became more functional.	Introduced raised hems and [...] for greater ease of movement.
Exploited the use of jersey fabrics formerly used for underwear.	The draping qualities of jersey suited her designs.
Used mainly neutral colours.	Created graceful, well-desig[...] garments.
Synonymous with the 'Little Black Dress' (LBD), introduced in 1926.	The simplicity of the LBD ha[...] made it an iconic wardrobe [...]
Designed the Chanel suit in 1954, using tweed sourced from Scotland, influenced by menswear.	The Chanel suit combined elegance, movement, minimalism and straight cuts, creating a modern post-war style.

[handwritten note: Punk – developed in the early to mid 1970's in US/UK australia form punk Rock music]

Table 2.2.8 Christian Dior

Christian Dior (1905–1957)	
French fashion designer renowned for creating shapes and silhouettes, who influenced new designers throughout the 1950s.	
Designer information	**Design work**
Introduced his 'New Look' collection in 1947.	The New Look featured boned, bustier-styled bodices and very flared skirts, creating a curvaceous form.
	These designs required new styles of underwear, such as corselettes called 'waspies'.
Revolutionised women's dress with the New Look and restored Paris as the centre of the fashion world after the Second World War.	Times were frugal and the New Look was criticised due to the amount of fabric the designs required.

Figure 2.2.7 Coco Chanel's Little Black Dress

Table 2.2.9 Mary Quant (A-level only)

Mary Quant (b. 1934)	
Welsh fashion designer and a British fashion icon who was an instrumental figure in the 1960s, London-based 'Mod' and youth fashion movements.	
Designer information	**Design work**
Opened her first shop, Bazaar, on the King's Road in London in 1955, selling affordable clothes to teenagers.	Encouraged young people to dress to please themselves.
Known for fun, easy-to-wear fashions.	Made use of synthetic fabrics, e.g. Crimplene and PVC.

→

Mary Quant (b. 1934)

One of the designers credited with designing the miniskirt in the 1960s and, later, hot pants.	Clothing was bright, with block colours and simple shapes, e.g. tubular or slightly flared shift style.
Focused on household goods and make-up in the 1970s and 1980s, rather than just her clothing lines.	Designed the interior of the Mini car in 1988. Author of five books including two autobiographies.

Table 2.2.10 Yves Saint Laurent (A-level only)

Yves Saint Laurent (1936–2008)

French fashion designer who became head designer at the House of Dior at the age of 21.

Designer information	Design work
The straight line of his designs in his spring 1958 collection created a softer version of Dior's New Look.	Gained international recognition with what would later be known as the 'trapeze dress'.
Regarded as being among the principal fashion designers in the 20th century.	One of the first fashion houses to open a boutique selling ready-to-wear fashion lines.
Was able to adapt his style to reflect the changes in fashion.	Wanted women to look comfortable yet elegant at the same time.
Introduced his iconic Mondrian shift dress in his autumn/winter collection of 1965/66.	Inspired by a painting by Piet Mondrian and reflected the important influence art had on his work.
In 1966, he introduced the 'Le Smoking' tuxedo suit for women.	The androgynous look was modified to be more feminine.

Figure 2.2.8 Trapeze dress by Yves Saint Laurent

Table 2.2.11 Pierre Cardin (A-level only)

Pierre Cardin (b. 1922)

Italian-born, French fashion designer.

Designer information	Design work
Founded his fashion house in 1950.	Introduced the '**bubble dress**' in 1954, creating a unique silhouette.
Best known for his futuristic, space-age designs of the 1950s and 1960s.	Used modern materials, for example knitted and heat-moulded synthetics, metallics and plastics.
Preferred 3D geometric shapes and motifs, often ignoring the female form.	Progressed into unisex fashions, sometimes experimental and impractical.
Launched a ready-to-wear collection in 1959 for a French department store.	As **haute couture** began to decline, ready-to-wear collections such as Cardin's became very popular.
A member of the Chambre Syndicale de la Haute Couture et du Prêt-à-Porter from 1953 to 1993.	Set the trend for 'Mod Chic' in the 1970s, by being the first to combine forms, such as the mini and maxi skirt, in a collection.

Key terms

Bubble dress: a dress design by Pierre Cardin with a cinched waist and rounded skirt resembling a bubble. Introduced in 1954, the shape became an international success and is still popular today.

Haute couture: high-end fashion that is constructed by hand from start to finish, and made from top-quality materials and components.

Table 2.2.12 Vivienne Westwood

Vivienne Westwood (b. 1942)	
British fashion designer and businesswoman	
Designer information	**Design work**
First came to public notice when she made clothes for her boutique in the King's Road in the 1970s (in partnership with Malcolm McLaren).	One of the engineers of the punk fashion phenomenon. Clothes designed to be anti-establishment, and decorated with political slogans and distasteful images.
Her design work and clothing ranges were inspired by the shock value of punk.	Products were often made in red tartan, black leather and plastic, and accessorised with spikes, chains and safety pins, or ripped and distressed and embellished with straps and buckles.
In the 1980s she moved away from punk, and became inspired by historical costume.	The Pirate Collection in autumn/winter 1981 celebrated the romantic age of pirates and highwaymen, and the 'mini-crini' in 1985 was inspired by early Victorian crinoline skirts.
Later collections were inspired by ethnic patterns of native Americans, New York graffiti and Rococo gowns.	The Buffalo Girls/Nostalgia of Mud collection in 1982 was inspired by Peruvian women wearing bowler hats and full skirts.
She first introduced underwear as outerwear in her autumn/winter collection of 1982.	Feminine designs focusing on 'erotic feminine features'.
Her self-taught tailoring skills allowed her to explore dynamic cuts and shapes, which she combined with her interest in British traditional clothing.	The use of traditional fabrics, for example Scottish tweed.
Much of her design work was influenced by her many political causes.	T-shirt slogans publicising political causes such as the Campaign for Nuclear Disarmament, climate change and civil rights groups.

Table 2.2.13 Alexander McQueen

Alexander McQueen (1969–2010)	
British fashion designer known for his creativity, originality and immaculate tailoring.	
Designer information	**Design work**
Considered to be one of the most influential designers of the 1990s and 2000s.	Often shocking and challenging, his early fashion shows earned him the title 'l'enfant terrible'
A skilled Savile Row tailor.	Created an impeccably tailored look.

→

Exam tip

Use sketches to illustrate your understanding of the work of fashion designers, making sure they are clear and include a back view. Add additional notes to describe the key features, including the materials used, for example tweed fabric, heat-moulded synthetics or black leather.

Alexander McQueen (1969–2010)	
Chief designer at Givenchy from 1996 to 2001, a period that included some iconic moments of his career.	In 1998, he controversially used double amputee model Aimee Mullins on the catwalk, with intricately carved wooden prosthetic legs.
Known for his spectacular, theatrical fashion shows, which often used extreme methods to showcase the catwalk outfits.	Exploited new technologies, such as using holographic images and robots to spray paint catwalk garments.
'The Highland Rape' collection from 1995/96 was inspired by Scottish culture and his own heritage.	Ripped bodices and hems, chains and models with entangled hair.
His **'bumsters'** design first appeared in 1996.	Initiated a global trend in low-rise jeans.

Key term

Bumsters: a low-rise trouser design introduced by Alexander McQueen in 1996, which led to a worldwide fashion for low-rise jeans, particularly among young people.

Now test yourself

TESTED

1 Why was Art Nouveau known as the 'Stile Liberty' in Italy during the Art Nouveau period?
2 Discuss the socio-economic factors that influenced the 'Age of Punk'.
3 Compare the types of fabrics that would have been used in the fashions of Art Nouveau with those used in the Pop Art era.
4 Describe the influences behind Vivienne Westwood's 'mini-crini'.
5 Investigate the clothes typical of Vivienne Westwood's Pirate collection. Identify and describe features associated with this collection.
6 Describe how Paul Poiret embodied the Art Deco period in his work.

Typical mistake

Make sure you can identify iconic designer collections and be specific when describing the influences, styles and trends within a collection. For example, Alexander McQueen's 'Highland Rape' collection, which featured ripped tartan dresses.

2.3 How technology and cultural changes can impact the work of designers

Socio-economic influences

REVISED

What people wear is affected by their lifestyles, outlook and expectations. Designers need to understand changing trends to be able to design successfully for individual markets. They often buy in information from trend forecasting companies to make sure their ideas fit with consumers' changing tastes. See Chapter 1.13 for more on trends.

Key term

Socio-economic influences: the social and economic factors that help to shape lifestyle, attitudes and expectations.

Major developments in fashion design and manufacture

Table 2.3.1 1900–1910

1900–1910: La Belle Epoque, or the Age of Opulence	
Socio-economic influences	**Trends**
Upper classes displayed their wealth through extravagant lifestyle. A strong class divide existed. Strict codes of etiquette governed most activities.	Upper/middle classes: ● Luxurious and extravagant dress ● Women wore several outfits a day ● Men also clothes conscious, but men's fashions had changed little from Victorian times
Technology included greater electricity provision and motor transport developments. Limited success in the emancipation of women. Women not expected to work, but more women being educated, participating in active sport. Many supported the suffragette movement. More liberal attitudes were spreading in artistic and intellectual circles.	● Children dressed in miniature versions of adult clothing ● Use of tight corsets, e.g. to achieve the S-bend silhouette ● Highly ornate clothes, delicate fabrics ● Long trailing skirts, large hats and gloves ● Paul Poiret was an influential designer of the period (see Table 2.2.6. Lower/poorer classes: ● Shabbily dressed ● Children often had no shoes ● People wore what they could get.

Figure 2.3.1 Dress from 1901 showing the S-bend silhouette

Table 2.3.2 1910–1920

1910–1920: a fashion-conscious era until 1914 and the outbreak of the First World War	
Socio-economic influences	**Trends**
An era of major social and political change. Class distinction through dress was less obvious. The generation gap widened. The First World War was a major influence on fashion. All classes of women adopted more practical styles. Many women joined the armed forces or took on war-related work. With men at war, more opportunities were created for women. Cinema became a popular form of entertainment. After the war, the rich and fashion conscious indulged in a sophisticated high life.	Paul Poiret's designs inspired many styles. Styles were better suited to an active, younger generation that needed easier-fitting clothes. Children's clothing followed the trend towards less formal, easier-fitting clothes. Men's fashions changed little in the early 1910s. Fewer fashions for boys as most were in uniform in their later teens. Radical changes in the silhouette of younger women's dress between 1912 and 1914 were considered shocking. The energetic dances of the period required looser-fitting dresses with shorter hemlines.

Figure 2.3.2 Chinosierie was popular in the 1920s, such as this Chinese tiger and cherry blossom embellishment

Table 2.3.3 1920–1930

1920–1930: the Roaring Twenties tempered by mass unemployment and the General Strike	
Socio-economic influences	Trends
Period of looser morals for the middle and upper classes, influenced by the entertainment media.	At the beginning of the decade there was an attempt to recreate romantic styles based on period costumes.
Social changes from the First World War spread more slowly to working classes.	A more modern, boyish look became popular, in line with a faster pace of life. The silhouette for the more fashion conscious was more youthful.
Most women expected to return to their pre-war roles, but there was a shortage of men. Many women had to provide for themselves, forced to take poorly paid work.	The chemise line dress became the main style. Very decorative fabrics were used, inspired by Egyptian, Chinese and Far Eastern motifs.
Women moved away from pre-war employment of domestic service into new jobs created in developing industries, e.g. banking.	Short hair and cloche hats went with the androgynous look. Accessories included shawls, low-heeled shoes, silk stockings.
This was a period of mass unemployment.	Simple shapes meant that women could make their own dresses, but mass-produced clothing became more readily available.
Young women found the post-war period liberating.	Simple, understated style marked a well-dressed woman. The poor still looked shabby, making do with cheap fabrics.
Women's drive for emancipation gained momentum: in 1928, women over 21 got the vote.	Women's participation in competitive sports gave rise to more casual styles, allowing freedom of movement.
Leisure pursuits grew in popularity. Foreign travel became popular, sportswear became more important.	Men's attitudes moved away from formal clothing. Trouser legs became wider. 'Oxford Bags' led to a looser cut with pleats for shaping.
	The female look became softer towards the end of the decade.

Figure 2.3.3 A cloche hat

Table 2.3.4 1930–1940

1930–1940: the effect of the Great Depression	
Socio-economic influences	Trends
The Great Depression, a severe worldwide economic depression, lasted throughout the decade.	Zippers became more widely used, replacing buttons.
Little money was available for new clothes and styles of dress among the different classes became more unified than ever before.	Beach pyjamas, cruise-wear shorts and bare-backed dresses became popular.
Women became adept at dressmaking and altering existing clothes. Home-knitted items were popular.	Lingerie included lighter corsets and suspenders.

Children's clothes were simpler and easy-fitting. |

1930–1940: the effect of the Great Depression

The wealthy still bought their clothes from couture houses, but the quality of mass-produced garments continued to improve and American-style department stores selling affordable ready-made clothes became popular.

Simplified versions of original designs could be manufactured and sold cheaply.

Radio and cinema celebrities such as Greta Garbo and Marlene Dietrich greatly influenced the way people dressed.

Royalty also influenced fashion trends.

The economic situation slowly improved in the second half of the decade, but the period was overshadowed by the growing threat of war.

Young men's fashions took on a more athletic look.

Fashion-conscious women were moving back to the hourglass shape of the Edwardian era but most women were wearing basic, practical styles.

Clothes became more stylish. Wide shoulders created a military look. Fur trims were a popular feature.

Dresses were made of silk and different grades of rayon.

Skirt lengths stayed short and practical for daytime; floor-length gowns were re-introduced for evening wear.

French designer Madeleine Vionnet popularised the bias cut.

Figure 2.3.4 A bias cut dress

Key term

Utility clothing: introduced by the British government during 1941 as an economic aid to conserve resources during the war years. Garment designs were modified to make them more efficient to produce.

Table 2.3.5 1940–1950

1940–1950: the effects of the Second World War and rationing	
Socio-economic influences	**Trends**
The Second World War affected daily life more severely than the First World War. Clothes/fabrics rationed from 1941 to 1949.	Women took great care of their clothes to make them last.
Clothing price controls the 'make do and mend' campaign and regulations concerning '**utility**' garments led to limited range of clothing available.	Female body profile was plain and square. Wartime fashion included siren suits, practical clothing, e.g. trousers and easily-matched separates.
More women in uniform as volunteers worked in male occupations while men were at war.	Menswear was influenced by American fashions and included trilby hats, jackets with well-padded shoulders and wide, straight-cut trousers.
The war removed many class divisions. Manufacturers realised the potential of the 'youth market'.	Girls wore pedal pushers as many cycled.
The huge need for mass-produced, affordable clothing revolutionised the fashion industry.	Dior's feminine 'New Look' line appeared in 1947, creating controversy with its generous use of fabric.
New synthetic fibres were developed.	

Figure 2.3.5 Early to mid-1940s ladies' suit

Table 2.3.6 1950–1960

1950–1960: a new, prosperous era overshadowed by the Cold War	
Socio-economic influences	**Trends**
The aftermath of the Second World War saw the reconstruction of industry and improvements in living standards.	In the early 1950s, women's fashion was figure flattering, influenced by Dior and Balmain.
Women returned to their pre-war status. The mature, elegant woman was a feature of the early 1950s.	Lingerie was greatly modified, creating a well-defined figure shape.
There were high levels of employment and an ever-growing market for modern clothes.	British designers Hardy Amies and Norman Hartnell.
	Conservative attitudes gave rise to tailored clothes for women.
The mid-1950s saw the rise of mass media in film, radio and magazines.	Tartan and twill trousers were a staple leisure garment for younger women.
Rock and roll music was popular, e.g. Elvis Presley.	Men's fashions inspired by British tailoring (the Edwardian look). The 'Teddy Boy' style evolved in young working-class males.
Youth-adopted crazes changed the shape of fashion for the rest of the 20th century.	Leather motorbike jackets, T-shirts, denim jeans and boots became a popular look.
Conformist attitudes were rejected by younger generation; anti-establishment attitudes grew.	The Beatnik style for girls included skin-tight jeans or short dark skirts, sloppy joe pullovers and heavy make-up.
Synthetic fabrics more widely used in the late 1950s.	

Table 2.3.7 1960–1970

1960–1970: enormous economic and industrial expansion and social change	
Socio-economic influences	**Trends**
Rapid developments in science, technology and space travel led to new fabrics/materials. Advertising promoted synthetic fabrics.	Big difference in the appearance of clothing from the early to the late 60s.
Opportunities for employment in the service sectors grew. Married women found it easy to gain work.	Tailored suits still favoured ('Chanel style') but easy-to-match separates and informal shapes became more popular.
Increased leisure time influenced styles of clothing.	New designers, e.g. Mary Quant, focused on young people.
Major social changes occurred. More girls continued into further education. The contraceptive pill was introduced and abortion laws reformed.	Models Jean Shrimpton and Twiggy epitomised young fashion.

Figure 2.3.6 Mary Quant wearing a shift dress she designed

1960–1970: enormous economic and industrial expansion and social change	
Changing attitudes and the more liberal approach were reflected in the media. The 'single girl' was quite typical of the era.	Trousers and trouser suits became popular.
Post-war baby boomers became teenagers, an important new demographic. New styles of pop music and colour photography in magazines had a big impact on teen fashion.	Skirts got shorter as the decade progressed. Women's dress predominantly either boyishly sporty or dolly-girl style.
	Tights replaced stockings. Heavy, low-heeled shoes with square toes were worn.
Designers André Courrèges and Pierre Cardin led the way in daring new designs, particularly for young fashion.	Leather, PVC and new easy-to-care for fabrics, e.g. Crimplene and Trevira, were popular materials.
Style became more important than quality. Young, trendy boutiques opened in Carnaby Street and the King's Road in London.	Men's fashions changed radically in the 'Peacock Revolution', led by youth culture, the Mods (Modernists).
	The romantic look of 1967/68 popularised velvet fabrics, frills/ruffles on shirts/blouses.
There was a move away from materialism. Young people favoured second-hand clothes as a reaction against cheap, mass-produced clothes.	The hippie movement saw the appearance of afghan jackets, floor-length kaftans, unisex fashions, long hair for both sexes.
	Easy-care fabrics were popular. Synthetics used for most children's wear. Waterproof nylon became popular.

Table 2.3.8 1970–1980

1970–1980: economic boom cut short by industrial unrest and high inflation	
Socio-economic influences	**Trends**
Fashion was less inventive.	Miniskirts continued to be popular.
Early 1970s were prosperous with a thriving consumer society. But high inflation after the 1973 oil crisis caused recession in world trade. Industrial unrest in the UK led to the three-day week to conserve resources.	At the beginning of the decade, hot pants were a big trend.
	Young people wore satin shirts, jackets and trousers, as well as original fur capes and coats.
	Platform-sole shoes and boots were widespread.
The rapid expansion in the fashion market created greater competition. Manufacturers cut costs by outsourcing production to developing countries (cheaper labour).	Trouser suits were worn internationally by fashion-conscious young women.
	Unisex fashions became more prevalent.
	Children's clothes were similar to adults'.

→

1970–1980: economic boom cut short by industrial unrest and high inflation

Socio-economic influences	Trends
Designers could no longer dictate fashion. Women decided for themselves what they liked, e.g. calf-length skirts quickly became passé, manufacturers with unsold stock went out of business. 1976 saw the rise of punk, a new youth culture that developed as a reaction to commercialism and unemployment.	Young men wore dandy-style clothes, e.g. kipper ties, fitted printed shirts, large collars. Blue denim jeans became a way of life. 1940s fashion influenced style throughout this decade.

Table 2.3.9 1980–1990

Figure 2.3.7 Donna Karan style

1980–1990: age of affluence with the rise of the Yuppies

Socio-economic influences	Trends
An affluent era with big wage earners, particularly in the finance business. 'Yuppies' were creating a new style. Diana married Prince Charles and initiated her influence on British fashion. Women became more career-driven and financially independent. Italian designer Franco Moschino mocked high fashion, influenced by Surrealist art. Some designers were questioning established ideas, e.g. Issey Miyake, Yamamoto, Jean Paul Gaultier. Sport and leisure also influenced fashion. Donna Karan and Norm Kamali designed more relaxed clothes.	There was a shift towards expensive, pretentious fashion; greater demand for designer menswear. Armani designed a softer, more relaxed style of suits for men and women. Female power-dressing styles symbolised women's success. Many new skirt shapes were influenced by historical costume, e.g. the mini-crini. Japanese designers introduced pioneering, modern materials and garment shapes. Jean-Paul Gaultier designed menswear influenced by gay culture. He dressed men in skirts and showed underwear as outerwear. Later in the decade there was a focus on comfort and amorphous style and the use of knitted fabrics.

Table 2.3.10 1990–2000

1990–2000: stock market crash, the Gulf War and the rise of the internet

Socio-economic influences	Trends
Stock market crash in 1987 caused recession in the 90s; less became more. Smaller disposable incomes curbed consumption, and fashion sales fell. Dress codes were relaxed. Street style, rap/hip hop culture and sportswear were major influences; clothes made from comfortable fabrics. Celebrities and the 'supermodel' influenced trends. This came with negative consequences e.g. rise in eating disorders among young women. Many people adopted minimalist, anti-consumerism attitudes to fashion.	Traditional ethnic clothing influenced fashion; there was a big push towards individuality. Softer, more subtle styles of tailored clothing were seen. The grunge look developed. Customisation grew as a trend, e.g. layered clothing and ex-army boots. Hip hop styles included half-mast jeans and baseball caps. Trainers had a big impact, e.g. Nike Air Jordans, Vans.

1990–2000: stock market crash, the Gulf War and the rise of the internet	
Concern over global welfare and safety influenced fashion, e.g. Lucy Orta's 'Refugee Wear'.	Issey Miyake's 'Pleats Please' collection and the use of environmentally friendly fabrics
Fashion reflected the socio-economic and technological progress of the time, e.g. the internet.	Cyber fashion included neoprene, polar fleece, rubber, PVC and high-performance materials. Deconstruction styles were influenced by 1980s Antwerp Six.

Table 2.3.11 2000 onwards

2000 onwards: terrorism and religious conflict, advances in new materials and manufacturing techniques	
Socio-economic influences	**Trends**
Designers are influenced by world events such as war, terrorism and religious conflict.	Due to technology, shopping is different e.g. internet buying.
Developments in technology have had a big influence on fashion.	Vintage has become a welcome and stylish change from contemporary garments.
Faster-moving fashion due to global trading and advances in manufacture and distribution.	Imaginative use of recycled materials.
New materials, electronics and finishes are being used.	Electronic components used, particularly in performance wear and for health purposes.
There is continued concern for the environment and sustainability.	Body-con.
Celebrity influence is still prominent.	Wearable GPS systems are now possible, and minute radio frequency identification (RFID) chips can be used to track a garment's manufacture.
New technologies facilitating more complex manufacturing techniques, e.g. seamless knitting, digital printing.	
New influences from cultural differences, e.g. African designers.	'Afterwords' collection shows one designer's humanitarian concern.

Exam tip

Don't forget to link to other topics to show your knowledge and understanding. Chapter 1.8 includes a section on inclusive design, which is relevant when you are answering questions about the trend towards more inclusive fashion in the 2000s.

Major developments in technology

REVISED

The introduction of regenerated and synthetic fibres during the 20th century

Synthetic fibres have been important in developing easy-care products.

Table 2.3.12 Examples of regenerated and synthetic fibres

Fibre	Development
Viscose rayon	Introduced in 1905 and made of **regenerated** cellulose. Called artificial silk, it was the first of the man-made fibres. Used for clothing in the 1920s and became popular again in the 1980s. A useful alternative to cotton.
High tenacity rayon and high wet-modulus rayon	Developed in the 1940s and 1950s to give improved fibre strength. New generation lyocell fibres are stronger, shrink less than viscose and have a reduced impact on the environment.

Key terms

Synthetic fibre: a fibre made entirely from synthetic polymers based on petrochemicals.

Regenerated fibre: a fibre made from natural cellulose that has been chemically modified.

➡

Fibre	Development
Nylon	Developed in 1935. The first synthetic alternative to silk.
Polyester	Developed in the 1940s and known as Terylene. Fibres came into general use in the 1950s.
Acrylic	Introduced by Du Pont in 1941 and known as Orlon and Acrilan.
Elastane fibres	Developed in America in 1950 and known as Spandex or Lycra. This elastomeric fibre revolutionised sportswear and underwear.
Microfibres	Developed in Japan during the 1960s. Ultrasuede was one of the first uses in the 1970s. More widely used since the 1990s in, e.g. sportswear and underwear.
Aramid fibres	Developed from polyamide in the early 1970s, e.g. Nomex, Kevlar and Cordura. Fibres are lightweight, strong and slash resistant. Used extensively for protective garments worn by the police and military.

The development of fabric finishes, e-textiles and smart materials

A product can be made more suitable for its end use with the application of a modern fabric finish. Modern finishes include chemical finishes and the use of thermoplastic fibres, which can be heat-set to give shrink- and crease-resistant properties.

E-textiles and smart materials were developed for use in specialised situations, such as in space or extreme weather conditions. They are increasingly used in everyday products to make life easier.

Further information can be found in Chapter 1.4.

Table 2.3.13 Examples of fabric finishes, e-textiles and smart materials

Finish or material	Development
Modern water-repellent finishes	Based on the use of fluorocarbons in preference to wax treatments.
Nano fibres	Used in a number of applications including: ● self-cleaning textiles and sportswear, and specialised clothing for safety and protection in extreme situations ● intelligent textiles that include electronic devices.
Interactive textiles	Textiles that include a microchip and circuit. Used in garments that need power to: ● keep a wearer warm ● operate lights for safety ● incorporate mobile phones, tracking devices, for example the O'Neill MP3 jacket ● monitor body functions, for example VivoMetrics life shirt.
Phase-changing materials	Materials that can change state from solid to liquid and vice versa. Micro-encapsulated in textiles, embedded in materials or used as a coating, they can store heat and provide heat-regulating properties, e.g. in ski boots.

Finish or material	Development
Impact-resistant textiles	Textiles such as D30 which have shock-absorbing properties. Used for protective sportswear, e.g. for motorcyclists or snowboarders.
Robotic textiles	Including robotics in textiles is a new area of development with many potential applications, such as protective clothing for those working in the military, rescue services, or in construction in dangerous situations, and for the rehabilitation of seriously injured people.

New methods of manufacturing clothing and textile materials

Mass production of clothing began only in the First World War when military uniforms in the same style and of a standard quality were required. The development of new fabrics such as rayon and the trend towards simpler garments meant that factory production methods were increasingly used to manufacture clothes.

Advances have continued since then, leading to the sophisticated mass-production methods we see today. Factors that affected this development during the 20th century include:

● the technical knowledge and skills that came over from America
● the availability of electricity to power machines
● the appearance of mass-produced goods for the working classes
● more efficient production techniques introduced by Marks & Spencer
● wider advertising through magazines
● the ability of mass production to make clothing and fashion available to all
● the effects of rationing after the Second World War, which meant manufacturing methods had to become streamlined
● competition from cheaper overseas manufacturers
● the development of CAD/CAM from the 1980s
● investments made in automated pattern design and fabric cutting equipment
● computer integrated systems to aid the planning and management of the manufacturing process, such as JIT and EPOS, allowing for a rapid response
● designers experiencing a wider variety of design inspiration and materials through global influences
● developments in communications technology.

New decorative techniques

Computer control is a significant factor in the development of decorative techniques. Complex weaving and knitting patterns and decorative effects can be easily created with the use of digital printing, laser cutting and computer-programmed embroidery.

Further information is available in Chapter 1.4.

Development in the care of textiles

In the early 20th century, the natural fabrics used and the many layers of clothing worn meant that caring for clothes was a difficult and laborious process. However, improvements in fabric technology, washing machines and laundry products, coupled with a move to more informal fashions, led to clothes being much easier to care for.

See Chapter 1.11 for further information.

Table 2.3.14 Developments in the care of textiles

Period	Development
1950s	Easy-care synthetics and fabric finishes were developed.
1950s and onwards	Electric washing machines and labour-saving devices become more widely available after the Second World War. Washing machines developed throughout the 20th century, from twin tubs to semi-automatic and then fully automatic machines that can wash, spin and dry.
1990s	Improved cleaning materials developed, including easy-to-use biological and non-biological detergents, stain removers etc.
2000s	Developments in nano-technology have led to hydrophobic fabrics, which can repel water-based stains, and self-cleaning fabrics, which can degrade organic matter when exposed to light.

Product life cycle (A-level only)

REVISED

The product life cycle describes the five stages a fashion usually goes through from when it is first designed until it finally is removed from the market.

Table 2.3.15 Stages in the product life cycle

Stage	Marketing implications
Design introduction	A new, exclusive style is created and displayed on the catwalk. Made from high-quality materials and custom fitted, the style is very expensive and is worn by celebrities.
Evolution	The style becomes popular, is seen in the media and becomes more widely available but remains high-priced.
Growth and maturity	The style is adapted and manufactured more cheaply, and appears on the high street. Copies are developed for different price ranges. Depending on its popularity, this stage may last for a season or for many years.
Decline	The style becomes less popular. Surplus stock is sold off at reduced prices.
Replacement	The outdated style is no longer available.

Figure 2.3.8 The product life cycle

Social, moral and ethical issues (A-level only)

REVISED

Social, moral and ethical issues change over time and affect people's attitudes and lifestyles.

Sustainable materials and ethical production methods

Designers and manufacturers have a responsibility to use sustainable materials and ethical production methods in every stage of a product's life cycle, from sourcing the raw materials to its end disposal, in order to minimise the impact of the textile industry on the environment.

This issue is covered in detail in Chapter 2.8.

Culturally acceptable products

We live in a multicultural society and today's designers need to consider the needs and values of specific groups of people.

This would take account of cultural customs, for example the use of colour and symbolism or the types of fabrics and components favoured in different countries or cultures.

Clothing also reflects the identity and interests of the wearers, for example their musical tastes or religious beliefs, or the influence of celebrities. Designers will look to communicate these interests and values in their designs.

Products that are inclusive

See Chapter 1.8, page 69.

Products that could assist with social problems

New products, fibres and fabrics are increasingly developed in response to social needs, for example homelessness, poverty or ill-health caused by natural disasters or war. The textiles used are often multifunctional, to cope with a variety of environments, for example:
- emergency clothing needs to be functional, genderless and affordable
- textiles for temporary shelters need to be lightweight, waterproof and able to insulate against extreme temperatures

Textiles are also increasingly used in medical applications, for example wearable electronics that monitor heart rate.

Fairtrade

Fairtrade sets social, economic and environmental standards for both companies and the farmers and workers who grow the food and cotton we love. For farmers and workers, the standards include protection of workers' rights and the environment; for companies, they include the payment of the Fairtrade Minimum Price and an additional Fairtrade Premium to invest in business or community projects of the community's choice.

The FAIRTRADE Mark certifies that the standards have been met by the farmers, workers and companies that are part of products' supply chains.

The six Rs of sustainability

See Chapter 1.11, page 80.

Upcycling

Upcycling is the process of changing an unwanted product or materials into something new. For example:
- fabric from a well-worn dress is used to create patchwork shapes for a child's dress
- a man's tie is deconstructed and used to create a novelty fabric
- denim jeans are deconstructed and reshaped to make a skirt.

> **Typical mistake**
>
> Be aware of and remember to list the positive aspects of ethical processes that have been developed in the textile industry. Too often the focus of written responses is the negative impact the textile industry has on the environment.

Figure 2.3.9 The FAIRTRADE Mark

Now test yourself   TESTED

1 How did men's clothing during the period 1900–1910 change from that seen in Victorian times?
2 Why was women's wear in the period 1910–1920 considered to be shocking?
3 Explain what was meant by the phrase 'Make do and mend'.
4 Describe the 'Teddy Boy' look and explain how this look evolved.
5 What is your understanding of the 'Peacock Revolution'?
6 'Wearable electronics can pose an ethical issue as well as a positive one.' Explain this statement.
7 Give examples of how Marks & Spencer was innovative in improving efficiency and quality in clothing manufacture.
8 What is your understanding of multifunctional clothing?

2.4 Design processes

Stages of a design process

REVISED

The aim of the design process is to create new and original designs. It does this by gathering information to inspire new ideas and finding the most effective way to make prototypes. It is a circular (**iterative**) process rather than a linear one, as further research and modifications will be carried out as many times as necessary to produce a successful design.

> **Key term**
>
> **Iterative design:** a cyclical approach to the design and development process.

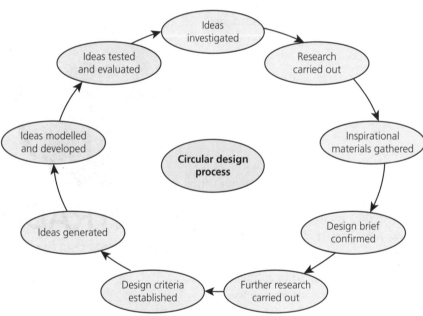

Figure 2.4.1 Circular design process

Investigations and analysis

Designers will carry out different kinds of investigations depending on:
- the context of the design
- the needs of the target market
- forecasted trends
- the need to consult with specialists
- an assessment of existing products.

The research gathered will depend on the context and may include:
● design features of former products
● mood boards to inspire a certain feeling or aesthetic
● the work of other designers.

The research data will be analysed to check that the investigations are relevant to the context and provide a good source of inspiration for possible designs.

Using inspirational materials

Mood or theme boards should be illustrated with inspiring images that will generate ideas for design work. Sketches and fabric samples can be included to evoke the design theme. You can see an example of a mood board in Chapter 1.14, page 89.

Ideas generation

Research analysis provides information that a designer can use to identify the design criteria. Design ideas to meet the criteria can be generated by:
● making quick sketches
● making more detailed drawings by hand or using computer software
● experimenting with fabric swatches, colours and textures
● sampling different working techniques
● trying out potential materials
● making 3D models out of paper, fabric or using CAD.

Although designers have to be mindful of their brief and the specification, they should also be prepared to take creative risks to generate innovative ideas.

Illustration

Design work is recorded in illustrations, which should communicate design concepts and final ideas.

Designers might include suggestions of textures, possible material combinations or suitable decorative techniques. They can also provide evidence of suitable manufacturing technologies, for example laser cutting and sublimation printing.

Modelling

Modelling is an important stage in the design process as it is used to test out ideas and firm up decisions about design ideas. The materials used for modelling are generally inexpensive and readily available, although sometimes a designer will test out a fabric that performs in a similar way to the final product, for example knitted fabric.

In the student example shown in Figure 2.4.2, the bodice has been developed in calico to establish the best way to manipulate fabric.

> **Key term**
>
> **Modelling:** the development of 3D shape, proportion and scale using paper, calico or computer software.

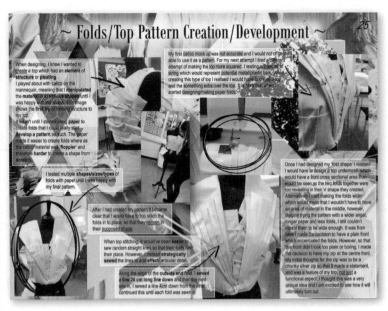

Figure 2.4.2 Modelling a bodice in calico

Planning

In the first stages of the design process many different ideas might be generated. These will be evaluated against the design brief, and the most promising ideas will be selected for further investigation. A development plan is put into place to keep the investigations focused on the design criteria and to work out how a successful prototype could be made.

In the development plan, the designer sets out the possible materials, components, techniques and processes needed for the design.

Evaluating and testing

The strengths and weaknesses of a design proposal can be ascertained by evaluating and testing it against the design criteria. This is done most effectively by seeking third-party opinions from clients, suppliers, experts and consumers. Their unbiased views will help the design team to judge the best aspects of the design.

Prototype development REVISED

Basic pattern/template drafting

The pattern for a prototype can be drafted by using:

- an existing commercial pattern
- block pattern templates
- pattern drawing software
- shapes traced from an original product
- moulage techniques.

The shapes are cut out by laying or tracing the pattern pieces onto the fabric and cutting around them.

Pattern notation and labelling

Universal symbols and technical terms are used to communicate information on pattern templates. The most common labels are shown in Table 2.4.1.

Table 2.4.1 Pattern notation and labelling

Pattern reference number	Identifies the design, for example, V1536. Commercial patterns will also include the manufacturer's name and perhaps a designer's name if it is an original design.
Section identification	Identifies the pattern piece, e.g. skirt front, trouser back, collar.
Grain line	Shows the direction that the pattern piece should be placed, i.e. along the fabric grain line parallel to the selvedge edge. ←——→
Fold line	Needs to be lined up with the fold of the fabric, creates a symmetrical shape when the pattern is cut out. ⌐——⌐↓
Centre back/ centre front	Shown by a dashed line that is midway between the shoulders. It is always a straight vertical line.
Cutting line	Usually a solid line. Multi-sized patterns will have different styles of line depending on the size, e.g. dash-dot-dash or a series of short dashes.
Balance marks/ notches	Balance notches are triangles cut in the fabric, e.g. for the placement of the curved edge of a sleeve to an armhole. Single notches indicate the front section of a garment, double notches indicate the back. In commercial production notches are often cut into the seam allowance to save fabric. This makes alterations difficult.
Adjustment lines	Usually two horizontal, parallel lines placed in the best position for lengthening or shortening, i.e. where it will not affect the shape of the garment.
Fitting line or seam line	Indicates the seam allowance, which is usually 1.5 cm wide unless otherwise stated.
Balance circles	Matching points, e.g. for pocket placements, sleeve alignment, matching points on a dart.

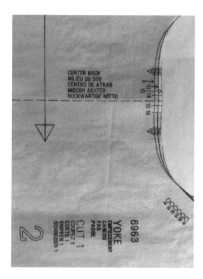

Figure 2.4.3 Pattern notation on a commercial pattern

Working from basic blocks

Blocks patterns can be used instead of commercial patterns to create the prototype pattern. Block patterns are commonly used shapes, such as skirt fronts or sleeves, which can be traced onto paper and adapted to create the desired shape for the prototype.

Block patterns don't usually have a seam allowance. This is because it is easier to add the seam allowance to the modified versions created for the prototype.

Basic adaptations to create unique and individual styles

There are several ways in which designers can adapt a pattern to create their own individual designs.

Table 2.4.2 Basic pattern adaptations

Method	Adaptations
Using pattern drawing software	Basic pattern blocks can be printed out and then the pattern can be developed and extended using dot and cross paper.
Using a mannequin	Pattern pieces can be tested on a mannequin to check certain features, e.g. the pleat position, and altered if necessary.
Using a commercial pattern	The existing pattern provides the basic shape, which can be redrafted into the desired shape, creating a new pattern.
Using existing products	Sections of an existing garment can be laid out and the shape traced to make a pattern piece. Each piece will require a seam allowance, which can be created using a **pattern master**.

> ## Key terms
>
> **Pattern master:** ruler with straight and curved edges for measuring shapes and seam allowances and drawing patterns.
>
> **Moulage:** moulding fabric around a mannequin to work out garment design and pattern pieces.

Moulage

Moulage is a method of manipulating fabric on a mannequin. Templates are developed from the fabric pieces draped across the mannequin. Fabric can also be draped across the body, for example to understand how the fabric folds and gathers. Moulage is a similar process to draping.

Moving darts and seams to create new shape

Darts are a method of disposing of excess fabric to create shape, for example around the bust or hip line. The size and position of darts can be altered to create good fit.

Alternatively, curved seams can be used to create shapes, for example princess seams.

Figures 2.4.5, 2.4.6 and 2.4.7 show how a pattern can be adapted by removing the dart and adding fabric fullness to the waistline.

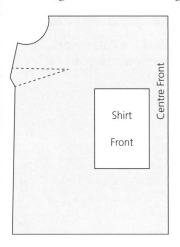

Figure 2.4.5 Cut pattern along lower dart line towards bust, and cut vertical line from waistline towards bust

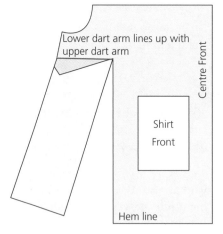

Figure 2.4.6 Pivot the section of pattern that is released from point of bust by moving lower dart line to line up with upper dart line

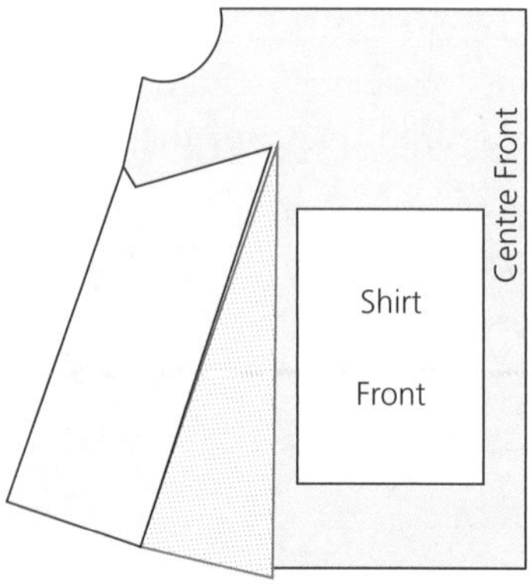

Figure 2.4.7 Insert an extra piece of cross and dot pattern paper into the gap to extend the pattern piece

Shaping or creating yokes

A yoke is a shaped section that is often placed at the back of a shirt or at hip level in a skirt. It is usually a double layer of fabric that supports the lower section of a garment, for example a gathered lower skirt can be set into a waist-to-hip yoke.

Use of toiles

A toile is a test version of a garment made up in cheap fabric, usually calico. Recycled fabric, such as old sheets, could also be used.

Toiles are made to see how the garment works and what further improvements are needed. They are usually made without fastenings and other components, or hems, as only the essential features need to be tested. Several toiles will be made throughout the design process until the design is finalised.

In the example in Figure 2.4.9, the student has tested the shape of her toile and decided to remove some of the bodice darts.

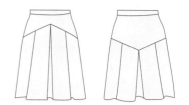

Figure 2.4.8 Skirt yoke

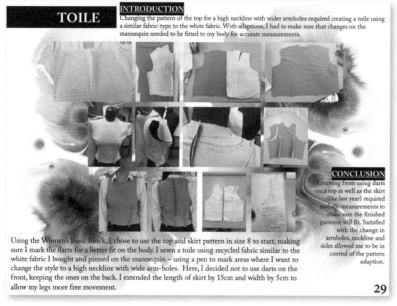

Figure 2.4.9 Example of toile development

The iterative design process (A-level only)

REVISED

Iterative design in a commercial context

In a commercial context, the design process is driven by the need for products to be:
- fit for purpose
- the right price
- appealing to the target market
- fashionable
- exclusive and original.

The design process will be iterative, with a continual cycle of sampling, testing, analysing and refining the design until the final prototype is ready for manufacture.

The use of different design methodologies when designing products

Different design methodologies are used to create new ideas or develop existing products. The methodology chosen will depend on the type of product, the target market, the client and the budget for designing.

Designers need to keep themselves up to date and will use the following sources of information to guide them:
- commercial trend forecasts
- catwalk and celebrity trends
- sales of current products
- trade shows, for example Premiere Vision in Paris
- social media, fashion magazines, trade publications.

Collaborative working

A design team with a range of skills will work together to create a final prototype.

Table 2.4.3 People that make up a design team

Team role	Responsibility
Freelance/in-house designer	Produces designs, illustrates and summarises the design requirements
Product developer	Plans how the design can be manufactured, and tests suitable fabrics and components that are available within budget
Pattern designer/cutter	Takes the design and creates a pattern
Pattern grader	Develops the pattern to provide a range of sizes in proportion to the original pattern
Sample machinist	Sews the first prototype using the pattern and according to the expected manufacturing process
Garment technologist	Ensures the product can be manufactured within budget, fits well and the specifications are agreed by the client.

The cyclic nature of commercial design and manufacture

The cyclic nature of the design process, the seasons and fashion styles all have an impact on commercial design and manufacture.

The cycle of development involved in testing a prototype before manufacture includes:
- testing it against the design criteria
- showing the design proposal to the client
- asking consumers for feedback
- consulting with experts
- providing a sample to exhibit on the catwalk.

Convention dictates that collections are produced in spring/summer and autumn/winter. These seasons often dictate the colour palettes and materials used, for example fresh, pastel colours and sheer fabrics in spring, and warm, dark colours and thick fabrics in winter.

Over the years, styles come in and out of fashion in cycles. However, variations in styles are now much more frequent as modern manufacturing techniques can respond to consumers' tastes and demands more quickly than before.

Now test yourself

1 List three different groups whose opinions could be surveyed in the testing and evaluation of design proposals.
2 Explain the process of moulage.
3 Only parts of a prototype may be tested when checking the fit of a garment. What sections of a jacket would you check and why? Explain your answer. Suggest the materials that would be used in this process.

2.5 Critical analysis and evaluation

How to critically analyse and evaluate

REVISED

It is important to appreciate the need for critical analysis and evaluation in order that possible improvements or modifications to a design can be made. Such assessments will establish the success of a design and its suitability for production.

See Chapters 1.8 and 2.1 for more on how critical assessments can lead to the development of new designs.

SWOT analysis identifies the strengths and weaknesses of a design. It also explores the possible opportunities for the design, and any threats to its success. Designers can use SWOT analysis to guide further development:

- **Strengths:** any features of the design that make the product unique or give it a competitive edge, for example the decorative details or the quality of the product.
- **Weaknesses:** any features that are inferior to other current products, or whether the product is suitable for the target market.
- **Opportunities:** what changes could be made to make the product more competitive or attract a different target market, for example using new technologies or modern materials.
- **Threats:** what are the possible risks that could adversely affect the success of the product, for example problems in manufacturing, changes in competitors' products, a change in demand, changes in attitude.

Key term

SWOT analysis: a process of evaluating the strengths, weaknesses, opportunities and threats of a business venture, project or product.

Exam tip

If you are answering a question on SWOT analysis, make sure you don't just mention the main principles of this method of analysis. Break down your answers into sections and use the headings to show your understanding in full, for example colour and type of fabric, construction methods, the range of components and fastenings, performance in use, position of styling details, cost.

Testing and evaluating products in commercial contexts

REVISED

Fashion and textile products need to be carefully tested and evaluated before they go to market to ensure they are fit for purpose and perform to required specifications.

Chapter 1.12 covers the testing of **prototypes** or the first versions of the design in more detail. Once the final prototype is produced, a commercial version will be made using production line techniques and processes. When this proves successful, 'the standard' is established. Future samples taken from the production line can be tested against this standard to ensure a consistent quality of product.

Key term

Prototype: the first version of a design to see it if works as intended, and to find out if improvements are necessary.

Specialised garments are performance tested in the laboratory or outdoors under the conditions they were designed to be used in, for example wearing a lightweight, waterproof jacket to go running in. See Chapter 1.1 for more on fabric testing and Chapter 2.10 for more on national standards.

Typical mistake

Remember to explain your understanding of the differences between workshop testing and industrial testing. There is a tendency for students' responses to focus solely on workshop testing.

Use of third-party feedback in the testing and evaluation process

REVISED

An objective, independent evaluation of a product can be gained through **third-party feedback**. This is valuable because it reflects unbiased views rather than those of the design team, and the product will have a greater chance of being successful as a result.

It is essential to get feedback at every stage of the design process. Feedback can come from:

- having discussions or conversations with potential customers in focus groups and customer panels (see page 100 for definitions)
- conducting short-question interviews (**quantitative interviews**) or more in-depth interviews (**qualitative interviews**)
- using marketing strategies, including social media, to encourage customers to review products

See Chapter 2.1 for more on quantitative and qualitative data and the use of focus groups and customer panels.

Figure 2.5.1 Testing fabric density to find out whether the fabric is windproof

Key terms

Third-party feedback: objective observations from people not involved in the design, creation or promotion of the product.

Quantitative interviews: facts and brief answers are collected from the target market during face-to-face or telephone interviews.

Qualitative interviews: feature indirect or open questions based on a topic, to get the interviewee to fully explain their point of view.

Now test yourself

TESTED

1 What is the difference between a waterproof product and a water-repellent product?
2 When does testing and evaluation take place in the development of a product?
3 How can social media be exploited in the testing and evaluation of commercially manufactured products?

2.6 Selecting appropriate tools, equipment and processes

Good and safe working practices

REVISED

Using the correct tools and equipment for specific tasks

Good results are achieved most successfully by selecting and using the correct tools and equipment. Different tools are designed and available for:

- measuring
- marking
- cutting
- sewing
- finishing.

In an industrial setting, specialised equipment is used at different stages, facilitating the efficient production of multiple products.

Workshop safety

Ensuring your own safety and that of others when using tools and equipment is paramount. See Chapter 1.9 for more on health and safety.

The effect of batch and mass production on the manufacturing process (A-level only)

Product construction and the methods used for manufacturing processes will be affected by the scale of production.

Mass production is the production of large quantities of identical products. This manufacturing system is highly mechanised and takes time to set up. It is an economical way of making products that require few changes, such as school shirts, but is too inflexible for fashion products that change frequently.

Mass production requires careful planning to ensure a steady flow of work through all stages of manufacture. Enough workers and machines need to be in place to complete each task so that there are no delays or hold-ups in the process.

Batch production is where teams work together to produce products. It is a more flexible method of production as workers are skilled in more than one job and can adapt their practices as fashions change.

See Chapter 1.6 for more on mass and batch methods of production.

Selecting appropriate manufacturing processes (A-level only)

The most appropriate manufacturing process will depend on:
- Product style and construction techniques: some parts of a garment may require specialist machinery (e.g. embroidered panels), other parts may require sub-assembly (e.g. collars, pockets).
- Type of fabric: some fabrics require specialist handling or processing techniques.
- Type of component: for example, piping or lace inserts in seams. When do they need to be incorporated and is any specialist equipment required?
- Order of construction: certain processes need to be completed first before others can begin, for example hems are generally completed after seams have been constructed.

Health and safety in a commercial setting (A-level only)

See Chapter 1.9 for details of health and safety and safe working practices in commercial settings.

Workforce training

- Jobs in the textile and garment industry are many and varied, ranging from machine operators, supervisors and managers to technicians, craftspeople and designers.
- Equally, the skills and qualifications required vary and include on-the-job training, apprenticeships, technical diplomas and university degrees.

> **Key terms**
>
> **Mass production:** the production of large quantities of identical products in highly mechanised factories.
>
> **Batch production:** a flexible method of production that enables changes to be made in product designs.

> **Typical mistake**
>
> Don't confuse mass and batch production. Both processes can be used to manufacture large quantities, but batch production is a more flexible method.

- Many skills are learned through first-hand experience working in the industry. Highly skilled workers will often train inexperienced workers.
- Although automated manufacture has replaced many types of workers, highly trained operatives are required to operate and maintain the machines.

National and international safety standards

See Chapter 2.10 for details on national and international safety standards.

Exam tip

Revisit Chapter 1.9 and make sure you know in detail employers' responsibilities for ensuring workshop safety under the Health and Safety at Work Act.

Now test yourself

TESTED

1 Give three examples of how sub-assembly may be used in the manufacturing process.
2 Watch the YouTube video 'British Clothing Company – Behind the Scenes' at **www.youtube.com/watch?v=2T3rteHTQ6U**. List and justify the use of automated processes employed in the shirt production shown in the video.

2.7 Accuracy in design and manufacture

Whether a manufacturer is producing a prototype or setting up a commercial production line, the efficient use of materials must be taken into account. Any waste material must be factored in to the costs of production, particularly as the financial and environmental implications of waste magnify as the scale of production increases.

Tolerances

REVISED

A high level of accuracy is required in production to ensure the final products are constructed according to the agreed standard and perform well. **Tolerance** is the level of accuracy acceptable in a particular situation.

- Tolerance levels are usually set within two measurements, for example between 5 mm and 15 mm, and are written into the manufacturing specification.
- Tolerance levels determine the accuracy of construction but will vary depending on the required performance of a product.
- Unlike other materials, setting very fine tolerances for textiles is less important as it can be difficult to achieve. Knits and fluid fabrics have a lot of give and change shape slightly during cutting and handling processes.
- However, finer tolerances are set for bespoke, made-to measure garments as a high level of precision is essential for the final fit.
- Low tolerance levels are set for the cutting and construction of sections that must fit together successfully, for example waistbands onto skirts.
- Other textile techniques also require smaller tolerances, for example sections that need to fit together for visual appreciation, for example appliqué.
- For some products precise sizing is less important, for example soft furnishings such as cushions and curtains are constructed to quite high tolerances.

Key term

Tolerance: the acceptable variation in the size of a product or part of a product, usually given as an upper and a lower limit.

Measuring and marking out

Measuring and marking out is a critical part of manufacturing. The more accurate it is, the better the quality of the final product.

Table 2.7.1 Factors to consider when accurately measuring and marking out

Factor	Description
Measuring tools	A variety of tools can be used including: tape measure, metre rule, set square, protractor, sewing gauge.
Pattern layouts	Pattern layouts need to be worked out to calculate the amount of fabric required, and to take into account the most efficient method of cutting out the pattern pieces.
	A commercial pattern will include pattern layouts for different fabric widths and to accommodate one-way designs and fabrics with a nap. The most common widths are 115 cm, 140 cm, 150 cm.
Matching fabrics	Fabrics with a nap, one-way designs, stripes, checks or repeating patterns will need to be cut in a particular way to ensure the garment pieces match up and the pattern is used to good effect.
	This will usually require extra fabric, which will increase the cost.
Seam allowance	If you have made your own pattern **templates**, you need to make sure you have included seam and hem allowances or allowed for them on the pattern layout.
	Seam allowances for domestic patterns are usually 15 mm.
	Seam allowances in commercial, large-scale production will be slightly less to allow for the more economical use of materials.
Cutting table	A large table or flat surface will help you to cut out the pattern pieces more accurately. You will be able to try out different arrangements of the pieces to achieve the most economical fit.
Tailor's chalk	A piece of fine chalk or pencil is used to mark fabric on one side. The mark is easily removed.
	An alternative method is to use tailor's tracing paper and a tracing wheel, but this can leave marks on both sides of the fabric, which are more difficult to remove.
Tailor's tacks	A temporary stitch is used to mark out seam lines, dart positions or balance marks. Double thread is used and the stiches are easily removed.

Key term

Template: a pattern used to transfer a design shape onto fabric to ensure accuracy in cutting.

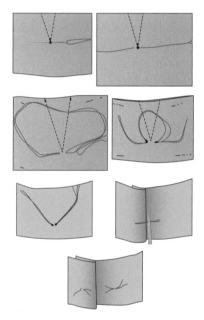

Figure 2.7.1 How to work tailor's tacks

Exam tip

You may be asked to calculate the quantity of fabric required for a layout plan. Make sure you show clearly how you have arrived at your final calculation. Use diagrams and do not forget the different standard widths of fabrics

Add the following—

Accuracy in manufacturing

Testing and the elimination of errors

In commercial manufacture, quality control (QC) checks are conducted at different stages of production to make sure the product matches the agreed standards. QC checkpoints can be written into the manufacturing specification to ensure a logical sequence in the manufacturing process, for example when epaulettes should be put on a jacket.

Each product can be inspected individually, but it is much quicker to check a sample of the products as they are being made. In the inspection process, samples are analysed and adjustments are made to rectify any problems. The reasons for the adjustments can vary, for example faulty equipment that needs to be fixed, machinists not producing the desired quality of work requiring further training.

Using measuring aids

Using a datum point and various measuring tools helps to ensure accurate marking out, which is essential if the pattern pieces are going to fit together properly.

A **datum point** is a fixed reference point from which other measurements are taken. For example, the fabric selvedge edge is the datum point for the straight grain line of the fabric. The grain line is usually marked on the pattern template. When cutting out, the pattern must be laid with the grain line parallel to the selvedge.

There are other possible datum points on fabrics. For example, with checked fabric, the datum point might be the centre line of the garment to ensure the checks match up on the finished product.

Measuring tools include:
- Pattern masters: a clear plastic ruler with curved and straight edges, used to draw pattern templates accurately.
- Set squares or protractors: used to measure and draw angles accurately.
- French curves: used to draw accurate curves, for example necklines or armholes.

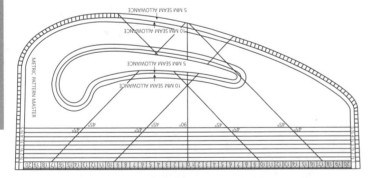

Figure 2.7.3 A pattern master

> **Typical mistake**
>
> Don't forget to explain why feedback about the manufacturing process is important. Give detailed examples of how manufacturers use sampling for quality control purposes, to show your understanding.

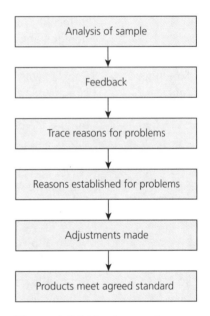

Figure 2.7.2 The inspection process

> **Key term**
>
> **Datum point:** a fixed reference point from which other measurements are calculated.

Now test yourself

1 Devise a list of six criteria that would be required for the accurate cutting out of pattern templates on fabric.
2 What are the three standard widths of fabric (in cms)?
3 Why is it important that shapes are cut out accurately, for example patchwork pieces?
4 What is the main advantage of vacuum packing layers of fabric for automated cutting?

2.8 Responsible design

Environmental issues

The production of fashion and textile products consumes vast amounts of natural resources, water, energy and toxic chemicals. This has negative impacts on the environment and on the lives of workers in the industry.

Sustainable fashion (or eco fashion) seeks to minimise these negative effects and is part of the growing trend towards sustainability in terms of human impact on the environment and social responsibility.

Sustainable materials and components

Designers and manufacturers have a responsibility to ensure products are made from sustainable materials and components. Examples of those that have a reduced impact on the environment are shown in Table 2.8.1.

Table 2.8.1 Examples of sustainable materials and components

Sustainable process	Materials/components produced
Recycling waste/reclaiming fibres	PET polyester
	Econyl
Organic fibre production	Organic cotton
	Organic wool
Sustainable sourcing	Bamboo
	Fairtrade cotton
	Fairtrade components
Closed-loop production	Lyocell
	Econyl
Modern fibre and fabric developments	Coloured organic cotton (not dyed)
	Biomimetic fibres
	Easy-care fabrics
Biodegradable fibres	Ingeo
Fibres made with reduced water consumption	Hemp
Fibres made with renewable energy	Fibres made in factories using solar, wind or hydroelectric power
Humanely produced fibres	**Ahimsa** (peace silk)

The packaging of textile products can also have a significant impact on waste. Designers and manufacturers need to consider:

- how packaging materials are sourced and transported, for example are they available near to where they will be used to save on fuel costs
- whether they are biodegradable and recyclable
- how storage can be minimised, for example by using JIT stock control systems
- whether carrier systems can be used to transport and store garments on hangers.

> **Key term**
>
> **Ahimsa:** also known as peace silk. Silk is produced humanely by letting the silk moths hatch out of the silk cocoon rather than killing them.

Conservation of energy and resources

The use of energy and resources in the textile industry can be reduced by making every stage of production more efficient. More up-to-date technologies can be used to combine processes, and modern developments in fibres can remove the need for some processes, for example dyeing.

How products are designed (A-level only)

Generally, textile products are designed to conserve energy and materials for economic reasons. However, advances in technology have made it possible to design more sustainable products.

Chapter 1.11 provides further information on this topic, including the six Rs of sustainability (page 80).

Reducing the impact on the environment

Fast fashion responds to consumers' demands for the latest trends. Production and distribution has to be rapid to keep up with this demand, as stock needs to be replenished quickly.

Fast fashion is discarded just as quickly, leading to a large amount of waste, which is incinerated or destined for landfill. Consumers should be encouraged to recycle more and products need to be designed with recyclable materials in order to minimise the impact on the environment:

- 'Cradle-to-cradle' clothing can be developed with components that can be recycled and fibres that can be reclaimed and reused in a **closed-loop system**.
- Zero waste materials can be used, for example **Returnity** and Infinity, which are made of 100 per cent recyclable polyester fibres.
- Natural fibres can be used which are biodegradable.

Raw material extraction

Designers and manufacturers need to consider the environmental impact of extracting raw materials for fibre production.

Table 2.8.2 Fibre production

Type of fibre	Source	Environmental concerns
Natural fibres	Plants or animals	Intensive farming
Regenerated fibres	Cellulose, e.g. wood pulp or cotton waste	Deforestation
Synthetic fibres	Non-renewable fossil fuels	Recyclability

Consumption

Responsibility for conserving resources lies not only with the fashion and textile industry but also the consumer. The post-consumer waste generated by fast fashion has a significant impact on the environment. However, there is a growing awareness that **slow fashion** is a more sustainable approach.

As part of the slow fashion movement, consumers are encouraged to buy:
- fewer, higher-quality clothes
- second-hand clothes

Key terms

Fast fashion: affordable fashion designs seen on the catwalk, which are then quickly manufactured and sold in shops within a very short timescale.

Closed-loop system: the solvent used in fibre production is recycled back into the start of the process.

Returnity: 100 per cent recyclable polyester fibres, used in clothing that is designed to be reused with zero waste.

Exam tip

Be aware of specific examples of products that have been designed or redesigned to reduce their environmental impact.

Typical mistake

Don't state an environmental change made by a company without explaining the benefit to the environment the change enables.

Key term

Slow fashion: durable fashionable garments that have a long product cycle.

- products made from organic, biodegradable materials
- products made from sustainable fabric such as bamboo or hemp
- products made from recycled materials or reclaimed fibres.

Consumers can extend the life of their clothing by:
- repairing and **upcycling** garments
- buying easy-care products
- storing garments carefully to protect them.

Consumers can support sustainable practices by seeking products that are:
- made by Fairtrade companies that do not exploit their workers
- made locally, which reduces the amount of 'fashion miles'.

> **Key term**
>
> **Upcycle:** to convert an unwanted piece of clothing or textile product into something useful and creative.

Ease of repair and maintenance

Designers need to consider how the durability of their products can be improved to make them more sustainable:
- Can the product be easily mended or repaired, for example by patching or darning?
- Are spare buttons, matching threads or beads provided with the product to replace worn-out parts?
- Are care labelling instructions provided to encourage users to wash at lower temperatures to conserve energy?
- Can fabrics be chosen to minimise the use of detergents and dry cleaning fluids?

See Chapter 1.11 for further information on the care and maintenance of products.

End of life

The impact on the environment of methods of product disposal needs to be considered:
- Incineration: toxic chemicals are released into the atmosphere.
- Landfill: materials and components can take a long time to decompose, methane gas is produced as a result and heavy metals can leech from metal items such as zips.
- Reclamation: biodegradable products break down naturally without releasing harmful chemicals, but if fabrics contain chemical finishes, reclaiming the fibres is more difficult.

Circular economy

A **circular economy** is a cradle-to-cradle approach to the product life cycle (see Chapter 2.3, page 118), whereby all the materials in a product can be continually reused through recycling and reclaiming fibres. Products should be designed so that they are easy to repair and care for to extend their useful life and made of recyclable fibres which can be used to make new products.

> **Key term**
>
> **Circular economy:** a continuous product life cycle through recycling or reclaiming fibres to make new products.

Sustainable manufacturing

Sustainable manufacturing:
- conserves the use of resources during production
- uses non-toxic materials and processing methods
- keeps waste to a minimum
- prevents pollution of the environment
- supports Fairtrade policies
- reduces 'fashion miles' in transporting products.

Traditional methods of fabric production use vast amounts of resources, but modern methods can reduce the need for water, energy and toxic chemicals. For example:

- Cleaning, bleaching, and dyeing natural fibres requires a lot of water and harsh detergents. Synthetics can be used instead as they are naturally white and clean.
- Dyeing microfibres in strong colours requires a lot of water. Dope dyeing synthetic fibres by adding colour before the fibre is spun reduces water consumption.
- Modern dyes have less impact as the chemicals used are less toxic, for example **azo dyes and pigments**. Natural fabrics can be bleached with sunlight or dyed with natural dyes made from plants.
- Sublimation printing, which uses heat to transfer the dye onto the fabric, reduces water use and effluent.
- Closed-loop processing systems and waste treatment systems can be put in place to reduce the polluting effects of toxic chemicals from a textile factory.

> **Key term**
>
> **Azo dyes and pigments:** bright chemical dyes used to colour textile materials.

Using alternative energy

Textile factories can reduce their use of non-renewable fossil fuels by switching to renewable and sustainable sources of energy such as wind, solar and hydroelectric power to drive their machines.

Methods of minimising waste

Material waste can be minimised by using:
- computer software to generate the most efficient lay plans
- automated manufacturing processes, which are more accurate and reduce the number of faults in products
- JIT stock control systems, which reduce over-ordering and the stockpiling of unnecessary materials.

Fabric waste can be minimised by:
- making sustainable capsule collections from left-over or recycled fabric that would otherwise have gone to landfill, such as H&M's 'Weekday's Remains'
- donating unwanted textiles to charity to be resold or exported for sale in developing countries
- reselling clothes, for example on eBay or at car boot sales.

Other solutions to minimise waste include using:
- EPOS systems to more accurately gauge the levels of stock required in a shop or the batch sizes for new items
- more local manufacturers to save on transportation costs
- the by-products of the cotton industry for other purposes, for example cotton seeds for cattle fodder.

The impact of waste, surplus and by-products created in the process of manufacture

Reusing material off-cuts

- Rather than going to landfill, off-cuts can be used in other products, or the fibres can be reclaimed by shredding the fabric and re-spinning the reclaimed fibres into new yarns.
- Off-cuts of expensive fabrics, such as silk, can be recycled and patched together to make one-off fashion items or accessories. This is known as 'pre-consumer recycled content'.

Chemicals

- Many processes in the production of textiles involve the use of toxic chemicals, from fertilisers used in growing cotton crops to bleaches and dyestuffs used in cleaning and colouring fibres.
- Unless carefully managed, pollutants can end up being discharged into local rivers, leeched into the soil or released into the atmosphere. This can damage the environment and affect workers' health.
- Cotton farming uses fertilisers and synthetic insecticides on a vast scale, which has damaging effects on the environment and workers. Although it has cost implications, organic farming of cotton would help to combat the amount of pollutants produced by the textile industry.
- Organic farming involves crop rotation, organic fertilisers and the exploitation of natural predators to promote pest control.

Heat and water

- Heat is required in many textile processes, for example to melt solutions, air dry fibres, heat water for dyeing and for steam-finishing processes.
- Vast quantities of water are also required for crop growing or to supply textile factories. Large-scale irrigation can exhaust local water supplies and lead to desertification.
- New waterless dyeing technologies are being developed that pressurise powder dye into polyester fabric using carbon dioxide.

Cost implications of dealing with waste

Managing waste and instituting sustainable practices is costly but it makes good business sense as satisfying the consumer demand for sustainable products will enhance an organisation's reputation. Responsible manufacturers therefore need to take into account the costs of:
- sustainable crop production and husbandry
- producing textile products
- waste management.

The impact of global manufacturing on product miles

Global manufacturing has meant that fashion products, materials and components can be sourced from anywhere in the world and therefore the distances a product travels during its life cycle have increased dramatically.
- Clothing and textiles make up about 7 per cent of the world's exports.
- Globalisation has led to lower prices, which has increased the consumption of cheaper, more disposable products.
- Manufacturers in Asia, and more recently eastern Europe, are better able to respond to the demand for fast fashion with smaller batches and shorter lead times.

However, concerns over the environment have meant that sustainable fashion has become a selling point. This has several benefits:
- Fashion miles are reduced as retailers use suppliers located closer to the point of sale.
- UK and European manufacturers no longer find it difficult to compete with Asia and eastern Europe.

Now test yourself TESTED

1 Explain your understanding of a closed-loop production system.
2 In what ways can packaging be modified to reduce waste?
3 Explain how modern production methods can eliminate the fabric dyeing process.
4 Explain your understanding of 'cradle-to-cradle' clothing.
5 How does the method of dope dyeing improve the use of resources?

2.9 Design for manufacture and project management

Planning for accuracy and efficiency

REVISED

A planned approach is needed for the accurate and efficient manufacture of products. The JIT stock control system is one way of planning efficiently. You can read more about JIT in Chapters 1.6 and 2.7.

Quality assurance (QA) procedures and quality control (QC) checks are also vital in ensuring that products are manufactured within budget and meet the agreed standards.

The impact of one-way designs, nap and pattern on fabric layouts

Designers need to consider the implications of using different types of fabric, as products with a one-way design, nap and pattern usually require extra lengths for cutting out. This can in result a great deal of waste.

Table 2.9.1 Impact of using fabrics with one-way designs, nap and pattern

Fabric type	Effect on the product	Impact on layout
Fabric with a nap, such as velvet	The fabric surface texture will look and feel differently depending on the direction of the pile, therefore the pile on the different sections of the product must all lie the same direction.	The pattern pieces must be cut in the same direction according to the nap.
Fabric with a one-way (repeat) design	The product will look wrong if one section is cut with the design upside down.	The pattern pieces must be cut in the same direction and cannot be grouped together to minimise waste. This will require extra fabric.
Fabric with a pattern, such as stripes and checks or a repeating pattern	The pattern on the different sections of the product should match up wherever possible, e.g. at the side, centre back or centre front seams.	The pattern pieces must be positioned along the length of the fabric to take account of the direction and repeat of the pattern. Larger repeats require longer lengths of fabric, which can result in significant waste.

Figure 2.9.1 Checked shirt with matched pattern repeat

Exam tip

Make sure that you are aware of the differences between napped fabrics, for example velvet, and one-way printed (repeat) designs for the purposes of calculating and cutting fabric. Repeat designs will vary in size and can significantly increase the quantity of fabric required. A maths-based question could be set on this topic.

Quality assurance (A-level only)

Quality assurance (QA) is about managing quality throughout the design, manufacturing and distribution processes. Completing products to the correct standard will ensure customer satisfaction and hence commercial success.

Every process contributes to the quality of the final product, so QA is the responsibility of everyone concerned. QA reduces costs because there is less wastage and re-working of faulty products. A consistent level of quality also enhances the reputation of the manufacturer.

Total quality management

Total quality management (TQM) is a management system designed to improve all aspects of QA by making continual improvements to business practices. Everyone in the company is involved in constantly monitoring and evaluating each stage of production in order to increase customer satisfaction and loyalty. The aim is to exceed customers' expectations to ensure repeat purchases.

Critical path analysis

Critical path analysis (CPA) is a management tool used to schedule the most efficient way of completing a project or process. It works out how different tasks should be sequenced in a production run to finish a process on time. CPA is used to:
- gain an overview of the whole production process
- help production departments meet schedules
- indicate how time is spent, so that possible improvements in efficiency can be made
- monitor tasks, which can highlight delays or bottlenecks
- manage costs, cash flow and budgets.

Scrum

The focus of scrum is to encourage teamwork between those working in different parts of a business in order to find the best ways to manage quality. Members of a scrum team will collaborate to improve QA in an organisation by:
- establishing quality requirements
- finding out where problems exist
- resolving issues that could affect the desired quality
- communicating with others not directly involved, for example suppliers
- taking responsibility for improving quality.

Six Sigma

Six Sigma is a data-driven business methodology that uses 'statistical thinking' at all levels. It involves the creation of a team of key people with extensive training in advanced statistics and project management.

The team takes an analytical approach towards improving quality and efficiency in order to reduce errors and defects, eliminate waste and lower costs. The target is to increase customer satisfaction and to build and maintain the skills and knowledge necessary to keep improving.

> **Key terms**
>
> **Quality assurance (QA):** the planning of procedures and policies that ensure good-quality products.
>
> **Total quality management (TQM):** a proactive approach followed by management and employees to ensure long-term customer satisfaction and loyalty.

Part 2 Designing and making principles

Quality control

Quality control (QC) is an aspect of quality assurance that involves methodically checking that products meet the required standards.

Samples are tested at regular intervals during the production process to identify any faults or errors being made. These can then be eradicated. Tolerances are checked to ensure products are being made accurately according to the manufacturing specification.

Table 2.9.2 Methods of quality control

Method	Description
Product sampling (A-level only)	This is a system of inspecting random samples from the production line. If defects are found that are outside the tolerances of the manufacturing specification, further inspections will be done. Faulty samples may be returned to identify and correct errors.
Quality circles (A-level only)	A quality circle is a small group of workers doing similar work that volunteer to meet regularly to identify, discuss and resolve work-related problems. The group is usually led by a supervisor who will present the group's solutions to management, but where possible, the workers will implement the solutions themselves.
Automated equipment to check for faults in fabrics	Computers and automated machinery can check for faults far more efficiently than workers. The checks are more accurate and faults are recorded automatically.
Labelling and quality assurance symbols	Logos or certification trademarks that provide a reliable and genuine guarantee of authenticity can be included on labels and packaging. For example, the certification trademark in Figure 2.9.2 shows that the product is genuine Harris Tweed, while that in Figure 2.9.3 shows the product meets organic production standards.
Quality control standards and voluntary codes of practice (A-level only)	See Chapter 2.10 for an explanation of national and international standards. Some standards are required by legislation, e.g. fire resistance in children's nightwear. Others will be voluntary but will appeal to customers buying the product, e.g. standards for sustainable production or quality assurance.

Key terms

Quality control (QC): specific quality control checks during manufacture.

Quality circle: a group of between six and ten employees who volunteer to meet regularly to discuss work-related issues.

Figure 2.9.2 Harris Tweed trademark

Figure 2.9.3 Global Organic Textile Standard trademark

Now test yourself

1 Suggest ways a production run could be scrutinised through a critical path analysis.
2 List the main differences between quality control and quality assurance.

Typical mistake

Don't confuse quality control with quality assurance. Quality control is just one aspect of quality assurance.

2.10 National and international standards in product design (A-level only)

See also Chapter 1.9 for more on national and international standards.

A **standard** is a set of technical specifications and guidelines that are agreed on and published in a document in order to improve the consistency and effectiveness of a particular product. For example, standard sizes are specified for bed sheets so that they will fit standard sizes of mattresses.

Companies who conform to an agreed standard can be trusted by consumers to provide reliable products, which contributes to their commercial success.

Designers and manufacturers are obliged to follow specific standards only if required to do so by legislation, for example under the Trade Description Act. However, there is a general obligation to provide 'safe products' as set out under the General Safety and Products Safety Directive that applies to manufactures, suppliers and retailers.

Products sold in Europe must comply with the CE mark (Conformitée Européenne), which certifies that they meet the requirements of European health, safety and environmental protection laws. Products must have a technical file explaining how the production standards are maintained.

> **Key term**
>
> **Standard:** an agreed and repeatable way of doing something, set out as a published document.

Figure 2.10.1 The CE mark

Garment labelling

REVISED

There are four areas of information that need to be considered when labelling a garment (see Table 2.10.1).

Table 2.10.1 Garment labelling

Fibre content	Compulsory in the UK under the Textile Products (Labelling and Fibre Composition) Regulations (2012).
	The main fibre types and their percentages must be listed in a way that is easily understood by consumers, e.g. 95% viscose 5% elastane.
Country of origin	Only required if consumers could be misled about the country of origin, e.g. a British flag made in China.
Care instructions	Not compulsory in the UK but strongly encouraged. Care labels help consumers keep their garments in good condition, which reduces the number of customer complaints and returns.
Flammability	Compulsory in the UK for nightwear and clothing for babies, toddlers and small children under the Nightwear (Safety) Regulations (1985). The label indicates whether the product meets the flammability standard BS 5722.

British Standards Institute

REVISED

The British Standards Institute (BSI) is the national standards body for the UK. It sets out the technical specifications for a wide range of products and services, and works in conjunction with the International Organization for Standardization (ISO) and the Committee for Standardization (CEN), which covers standards in Europe.

International Organization for Standardization

The International Organization for Standardization (ISO) is an independent, non-governmental organisation made up of the national standards bodies from 162 countries. The UK representative is the BSI.

It implements internationally recognised standards, which facilitates access to foreign markets and helps the development of global trade. An ISO mark provides assurance that the product meets universally agreed standards of safety and reliability.

European ecolabel

The European ecolabel identifies products that have a reduced environmental impact throughout their life cycle. This voluntary label was established in 1992 and is awarded to companies that conform to strict environmental criteria.

Packaging directives

The EU Directive on Packaging and Packaging Waste passed in 1994. EU member states are set compulsory targets to reduce and recycle packaging so that the environmental impacts of packaging are reduced over the life cycle of the product.

The objectives of the directive are to:
- minimise packaging weight and volume
- reduce the amount of heavy metals in packaging to reduce the toxic impact on landfill sites or during incineration
- introduce reusable or recoverable packaging designs.

The directive was revised in 2014 and new minimum targets were set for recovery and recycling – 55 per cent by weight of all packaging waste is now to be recycled.

Further revision in 2015 stopped large retailers from providing free plastic bags. Planned legislation suggests that plastic bag charges could rise and be extended to smaller shops.

Figure 2.10.2 European ecolabel

> ### Exam tip
>
> Be aware of current issues in the news with regard to the environmental effects of the textile industry, such as chemicals processes used in manufacturing yarns, as they can be used as examples in your answer.

> ### Typical mistake
>
> Don't write in general terms. For example, if you are answering a question on the disposal of textile products, explain and provide detail on how products could be recycled or reused.

Now test yourself

1 Explain what a technical file would include to satisfy the CE marking requirements.
2 What areas have the biggest environmental impact in the product life cycle of a textile product?

Exam practice

1 Explain the following terms and their importance in the manufacture of fashion products:
   a Manufacturing specification.
   b Gold seal standard.
2 Care labels use a set of internationally recognised symbols. Draw and name the five basic symbols that cover the main areas of care and maintenance of textile products.
3 Explain the meaning of the term 'circular economy' and give reasons why a circular economy is important.
4 Garments need to be shaped so that they fit the human figure. One way of shaping a garment is shown on the diagram below.
   a Name the method used.
   b Name three further ways fabric can be given shape so that it fits a human figure.

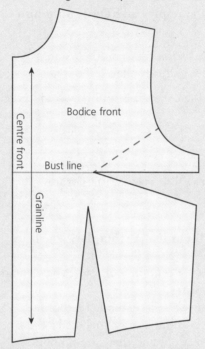

5 Explain the term 'feasibility study' and name two ways in which a feasibility study can be carried out.
6 Explain how designers might use each of the following:
   a Feedback from market research.
   b A prototype.
7 a Explain the difference between primary and secondary research in the design process.
   b Explain how three methods of primary research might be used in the design of snowboarding gloves.
8 The labelling and packaging of textile products provides important information. Give three different types of information found on the labelling of textile products.
9 Explain the meaning of the terms 'aesthetics', 'ergonomics' and 'anthropometrics' when designing products and prototypes.
10 (A-level only) The graph shows the stages in the life cycle of a fashion product. Provide the missing information in the boxes and explain stages B, C and D.

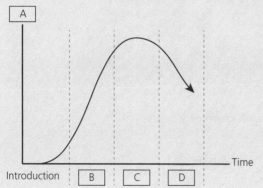

ONLINE

Success in the examination

AS-level

If you are completing AS-level Fashion and Textiles:

- you will take **one** written exam worth **80 marks** (this is 50 per cent of your total AS-level mark)
- the exam will last for **1 hour 30 minutes**
- you will be tested on **Technical Principles** and **Designing and Making Principles.**

There will be a mixture of different question types on the exam paper, including multiple choice, short answer and extended response.

In 15 per cent of the paper, maths and science skills will be tested in the context of design and technology.

A-level

If you are completing an A-level, you will sit **two** written exams.

Paper 1

- In Paper 1, you will be tested on **Technical Principles**, which are covered in Chapters 1.1–1.14 of this book.
- The paper is worth **120 marks** (30 per cent of your total A-level mark).
- The exam will last **2 hour 30 minutes.**
- There will be a mixture of short answer and extended response questions. Multiple choice questions could also be included.
- The paper does not have separate sections and there are no optional questions.
- Maths and science skills in a design and technology context will also be examined as part of this paper.

Paper 2

- In Paper 2, you will be tested on **Designing and Making Principles**, which are covered in Chapters 2.1–2.10 of this book.
- The paper is worth **80 marks** (20 per cent of your total A-level mark).
- The exam will last **1 hour 30 minutes**.
- There will be a mixture of short answer and extended response questions. Multiple choice questions could also be included. There will be no optional questions.

Paper 2 is divided into two sections:

- Section A: Product analysis
  - ○ 30 marks are available for this section. There will be up to six short answer questions based on visual stimulus of product(s).
- Section B: Commercial manufacture
  - ○ 50 marks are available for this section. There will be a mixture of short answer and extended response questions.

Maths and science skills in a design and technology context will also be examined as part of this paper.

Sample examination questions

Paper 1 (Technical principles)

> **Example 1**
>
> Modern and technical materials are new materials or materials that have been developed through the invention of new or improved processes. Explain the reasons why polyamide and polyester fibres are frequently developed or combined with other fibres to make modern and technical materials suitable for sportswear. Give examples of specific materials in your answer. (12 marks)

Candidate response 1

REVISED

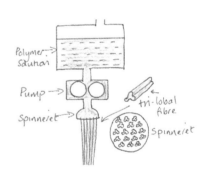

Polyester and polyamide fibres have many good properties such as durability, strength and abrasion resistance when used to make materials or fabrics with crease resistance or that dry quickly and are easy care. Because they are synthetic, their cross-sections can be changed to give them more properties.

In sportswear, the fibre could be engineered to be tri-lobal shaped so that it has less contact with the skin, improving comfort and freedom of movement. Changing the holes in the spinneret during the spinning process does this.

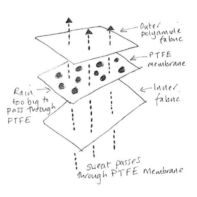

An example of a modern material used in sportswear is Gore-Tex. This is a breathable, laminated material that is waterproof due to its PTFE fine membrane. When using polyester or polyamide in combination with the membrane, it creates the perfect material for winter or outdoor sports as it is strong, lightweight, breathable and waterproof. Sympatex is another modern material that works in the same way and protects the wearer from the wind.

Another development in materials using polyester and polyamide fibres is Polartec fabrics. Polartec is very warm, lightweight and windproof, and has breathability, stain resistance and crease resistance. Polartec is a modern fabric that has really changed the way that functionality has come into clothing.

Polyester and polyamide are also cheap to manufacture and can come from recycled sources, making them good for the environment. They can be blended with a more expensive fibre to make fabrics suitable for sportswear. Blending the fibres means that less of the expensive fibre is needed, as the other fibres are the cheap polyester/polyamide fibres. The blended fibre fabric will then have the desired properties of both the polyester/polyamide fibre and the more expensive fibre.

Candidate response 2

Polyamide and polyester fibres are suitable for modern and technical materials used for sports. Polyester is good for this as its cheap so it will be cheap to make and buy, which is good for those with a limited income. They are both soft next to the skin which makes it comfortable to wear as it won't irritate the skin. This is good as the consumer can concentrate on the sport without being uncomfortable.

Polyester is breathable which makes it comfortable. They both have a little 'give' which means easy movement is allowed. Both are easy to care for so won't cost a lot in terms of time or money to look after – due to a lot of falls when doing sports, clothes can get can get dirty and need to resist stains. As they are breathable, they can absorb perspiration, which makes it comfortable to wear. Both fibres are very strong and hardwearing which makes the fabrics long lasting, which is good as it needs to be durable due to falls in sports. Polyamide is resistant to abrasion which makes it useful for sports such as skiing when consumers are likely to fall a lot. It does not crease easily so won't need ironing and gives the consumer more time for sports.

Paper 2 (Designing and making principles)

Example 1

In a global market it is important for the manufacturers of textile products to maintain levels of quality. Explain why quality assurance (QA) is important in the manufacture of textile products and the implications QA has for manufacturers. Include descriptions of systems and procedures associated with QA in your answer. (12 marks)

Candidate response 1

REVISED

Quality assurance is when quality is manufactured into the garment rather than checking for it afterwards, which is quality control (QC). Quality is important in the production of textiles so that products last longer and are more sustainable, with a longer product life rather than fast fashion, which does not last long. Making quality products helps manufacturers keep existing customers and obtain new customers. The British Standards Institute (BSI) is an organisation which ensures quality is guaranteed in products by supplying set standards to manufacturers which they must conform to if they want to use the BSI name. Using BSI standards is beneficial for manufacturers as it provides trust and helps ensure regulatory compliance by the manufacturer. BSI tests can be undertaken such as durability, which assures the consumer that the product is hardwearing and will last a long time.

Manufacturers also use QC checks and systems such as total quality management (TQM). This means that it is the responsibility of everyone in the company to ensure high quality in the product and not just the responsibility of workers on the production line. TQM ensures quality right from the start and not just by checking products at the end. QA proves a manufacturer's commitment to quality but there are some implications for the manufacturer in using QA. For example, some of the equipment and training needed are expensive. BSI tests have to be bought if the manufacturer wants to use them and these are expensive and take time to carry out. This makes product lead times longer and reduces profit.

Candidate response 2

REVISED

The company has to make sure that the products they make are of a satisfactory quality to sell them, and to check this they must comply with QA. QA means that the product is fit for purpose and includes everything that is needed in its specification. QA officers are given the job of checking over the completed products because QC checks would be done throughout the manufacturing process. The officer checks the product's appearance and quality. At this stage many different checks have to take place, for example seams, fabric and sizing. There are many implications in having a QA process. Checking products takes a lot of time to do. If a product is not made well and is bad quality, it could mean that the rest of the products in the batch could also be bad quality. If the products do not reach the QA standards set by the company they cannot be sold and the company will lose money.

Assessment comment

The student shows good understanding of QA with some examples of relevant systems. There is some reference to what QA means for the manufacturer although there is a lack of clarity in places. There are references to BSI standards but few examples are given of specific standards. This response would be placed at the top of the mid-mark range. It could be improved with more examples of QA systems and more clarity about the implications for the manufacturer, and examples of specific QC checks.

Assessment comment

This is a weaker response, which lacks understanding of the difference between QA and QC. There are references to QC checks but these are not explained in any detail and there is little evidence that the student understands the implications for the manufacturer. It would be placed in the lower mark band. The response could be improved with an explanation of what is meant by QA as distinct from QC, the inclusion of QA systems and more accurate references to the implications for the manufacturer, and clearer details about relevant QC checks.

Glossary

Absorbency: a fabric's ability to retain moisture; it affects a fabric's comfort, ease of care, dye-ability and static build-up.

Abstract: a brief summary of the report, which helps the reader quickly grasp the content.

Adaptive clothing: products designed to meet the needs of people with poor mobility and dexterity.

Aesthetics: the beauty or tastefulness of the look of a product, and how attractive it is to the consumer.

Ahimsa: also known as peace silk. Silk is produced humanely by letting the silk moths hatch out of the silk cocoon rather than killing them.

Anthropometrics: scientific measurements of the human body applied to the design of products.

Anti-bacterial: prevents the development of bacteria.

Anti-microbial: kills or inhibits the growth of microorganisms.

Art Deco: a style of visual arts, architecture and design that first appeared in France before the First World War featuring modern geometric designs.

Art Nouveau: an international style of decorative art, architecture and applied art inspired by organic shapes and structures.

Azo dyes and pigments: bright chemical dyes used to colour textile materials.

Batch production: a flexible method of production that enables changes to be made in product designs.

Bespoke products: products designed and manufactured to individual specifications.

Body scanner: captures measurements and the shape of a customer's body to produce a highly accurate 3D digital body form.

Brand identity: the distinctive and memorable style, ethos and values of a business.

British Standards Institute (BSI): a national organisation that devises agreed standard procedures for performing a wide range of tasks.

BSI Kitemark: a quality mark to show that a product conforms to agreed standards.

Bubble dress: a dress design by Pierre Cardin with a cinched waist and rounded skirt resembling a bubble. Introduced in 1954, the shape became an international success and is still popular today.

Bumsters: a low-rise trouser design introduced by Alexander McQueen in 1996, which led to a worldwide fashion for low-rise jeans, particularly among young people.

Chitosan: a naturally sourced anti-bacterial found in the shells of crustaceans such as crabs.

Circular economy: a continuous product life cycle through recycling or reclaiming fibres to make new products.

Closed-loop system: the solvent used in fibre production is recycled back into the start of the process.

Code of practice: a voluntary set of rules agreed by a professional body that guide a company's way of working.

Colour fastness: the ability of a fibre or fabric to retain dye fastness during manufacturing processes and when washed or exposed to sunlight.

Computer-aided administration (CAA): systems used to plan and carry out all aspects of administration.

Computer-integrated manufacture (CIM): the term used to describe how computers are used to oversee all stages of bringing a product to market.

Computer numerical control (CNC): a program, converted from CAD files, which uses special codes to control CAM equipment.

Consumer Rights Act (2015): an act which simplifies consumer protection law and reflects the changing ways that consumers buy goods and services.

Control: a sample that is untreated or unchanged.

Control of Substances Hazardous to Health Regulations (COSHH): legislation to prevent, reduce or control people's exposure to hazardous substances in the workplace.

Copyright: unregistered rights that protect original works such as books, plays, artwork, illustrations or photographs.

Corporate identity: the visual representation of the business, for example through the use of logos and trademarks.

Cure: a heat process used to fix dyes and chemical finishes on fabrics.

Customer panels: a group of prospective customers who are frequently consulted on their opinions about a new product during the different stages of development.

Datum point: a fixed reference point from which other measurements are calculated.

Degradation: the gradual breakdown of a dye, leading to loss of colour in a product.

Demand-activated manufacture: uses digital technology to produce fashion products on demand as customers order them.

Demographics: a study of population statistics, for example age, gender, marital status, income and occupation.

Denier: a measure of thickness used for all filament yarns. The higher the denier number, the thicker the yarn.

Design right: gives automatic protection to the appearance of a product but only provides some legal protection for designers to stop unauthorised copying.

Directional fabric: fabric that has a definite one-way pattern or nap.

Directional pile: the raised surface on a fabric that appears to change colour when viewed from different angles.

Disassembly: to take apart step-by-step, or to deconstruct.

Drape: the way a fabric hangs or falls.

Draping: the process of arranging and pinning fabric on a mannequin to develop the shape of a garment. After arranging, the fabric is removed and used to create the pattern for construction.

Dye fastness: the ability of a fibre or fabric to retain dye.

Dye liquor: a solution containing dyestuff, water and chemicals (if needed to help the dye bind to fibres).

Dye sublimation printing: when heat and pressure turn special dyes from a solid into a gas and then back into solid again once it has transferred from paper and bonded with synthetic fabric.

Dyestuff: an organic or inorganic coloured substance used to add colour to textile materials.

Elasticity/extensibility: the measure of how much a fabric will stretch and extend.

Electronic data interchange (EDI): a system that allows computers to exchange information electronically in a standard format between business partners.

Electronic point of sale (EPOS): a self-contained electronic checkout that also updates stock levels.

Empathic design: user-centred design approach that considers the user's feelings towards products.

Entrepreneur: a person who demonstrates initiative and invests capital into an idea by setting up a business, project or other venture.

Enzyme: a substance produced by a living organism, which acts as a catalyst to bring about a specific biochemical reaction.

Ergonomics: the relationship between people and the products they use.

Eutrophication: excessive richness of nutrients in a lake or other body of water caused by the phosphates found in laundry detergents as well as fertilisers used on plants. May result in oxygen depletion of the water.

Fashion cycle: how a fashion trend begins, becomes popular, becomes unfashionable, then disappears.

Fauvism: a style of art that emphasised the use of strong colour over representation or realistic values.

Feed dogs: the metal teeth-like ridges that move in and out of the metal plate below a sewing machine's needle and presser foot.

Fibre: a fine, hair-like thread.

Fibre extrusion: the process where fluid, molten, man-made fibre polymer (dope) is pushed through the holes in the nozzle part of a spinning machine to create filament fibres.

Finishing process: an additional process to improve the appearance and/or performance of a fabric.

Focus group: a panel of consumers who rate the product and feed back their opinions. Those taking part will be from the target group.

Formability: the ability to manipulate and shape fabrics without damaging them.

Furniture and Furnishings (Fire Safety Amendment) Regulations (1993): set levels of fire resistance for fabric coverings used in upholstered furniture and furnishings.

The garçonne look: a slim style of clothes giving a boyish silhouette, popular in the 1920s.

Gender stereotypes: over-generalisations about the characteristics of people based on their gender.

General Product Safety Regulations (2005): place a responsibility on businesses to supply safe goods.

Greige or **loomstate:** terms used for a fabric in its natural state as it comes from the loom or the knitting machine.

Grey scale cards: used to show differences in colour intensity when comparing control samples with samples exposed to washing and UV light.

Handle: how a fabric feels when touched.

Harem pantaloons: a Turkish-style trouser with narrow ankles introduced into western fashion by Paul Poiret in about 1910.

Haute couture: high-end fashion that is constructed by hand from start to finish, and made from top-quality materials and components.

Hazard: a danger or risk that can cause someone harm.

Health and Safety at Work Act (1974): the primary legislation for British health and safety law.

Health and Safety Executive (HSE): a national independent watchdog for work-related health, safety and illness.

Histogram: a chart with bars used to show the distribution of numerical data.

Hydrophilic: having a strong attraction for water, i.e. water-loving.

Image mapping: allows a designer to show how a pattern or colour might look on a garment.

Inclusive design: designing products for ease of use by the maximum possible range of people.

Intellectual property (IP): ideas, artistic work or physical creations that are entitled to protection for the originator in the form of copyright, design rights, patent, registered design or trademark.

Intellectual Property Office (IPO): the official UK government body responsible for IP.

Intellectual property rights (IPR): the legal protection of IP.

Iterative design: a cyclical approach to the design and development process.

Jacquard fabrics: fabrics where the pattern is created through weaving or knitting rather than being printed onto the fabric.

Just-in-time (JIT): a stock-control management system that ensures fabrics and components arrive at the factory just as they are needed to go onto the production line.

Lay plan: a diagram showing how pattern templates are to be placed onto fabric ready for cutting out.

Lead time: the time between the start and completion of a production process.

Logo: an instantly identifiable graphic symbol or design used alongside a trademarked brand identity.

Lustre: a natural sheen that gives shine to a fibre.

Mass production: the production of large quantities of identical products in highly mechanised factories.

Microencapsulated fibre: a microfibre that has tiny capsules containing health or cosmetic chemicals embedded into its hollow centre.

Microfibre: an extremely fine synthetic fibre.

Modelling: the development of 3D shape, proportion and scale using paper, calico or computer software.

Modern material: a material that has been developed through the invention of new or improved processes.

Moulage: moulding fabric around a mannequin to work out garment design and pattern pieces.

Multi-fibre swatch: a narrow band of woven fabric containing separate segments of acetate, cotton, nylon, polyester, acrylic and wool fibres. It is used to demonstrate the uptake of dye staining when washing different types of fabric.

Nano-fibre: an extremely lightweight strong fibre that is less than one micron in diameter.

Nap: a raised surface made by brushing the fabric surface after weaving.

Natural fibre: a fibre that comes from a natural cellulose (plant) or protein (animal) source.

Non-woven fabric: made directly from fibres.

Pantone: a standardised colour matching system.

Patent: legal protection for inventions relating to the way in which a product functions.

Pattern design system (PDS): a computer program that makes pattern templates automatically from a 3D model.

Pattern grading: pattern designers use anthropometric and ergonomic data to grade patterns for different sizes.

Pattern master: ruler with straight and curved edges for measuring shapes and seam allowances and drawing patterns.

Percentiles: a specific statistical percentage range, often used to define appropriate anthropometric data for design purposes.

Performance codes: the technical requirements for a product, material or process to be fit for its intended purpose.

Photochemically produced screens: screen's mesh is coated with soluble photosensitive chemicals. Areas to be printed are blocked off to stop them becoming insoluble when exposed to UV light. Washing removes still soluble chemicals from blocked areas; print paste passes through mesh.

Pile weaves: classified as three-yarn system weaves as a third yarn is woven in with the warp and weft to make a fabric with a raised surface.

Polymer: a long chain of molecules made up of fibre-forming atoms that are linked together.

Pop Art: an art movement inspired by popular culture that emerged in Britain and America in the mid to late 1950s.

Presentation board: a collection of illustrations, samples and colourways used to present final ideas to a client.

Prêt-à-porter: ranges of designer clothes sold ready to wear rather than made to measure.

Primary data: research carried out to collect new information.

Production planning and control (PPC): a system used to plan and control all aspects of manufacturing including quality control.

Prototype: the first version of a design to see it if works as intended, and to find out if improvements are necessary.

Qualitative interviews: feature indirect or open questions based on a topic, to get the interviewee to fully explain their point of view.

Quality assurance (QA): the planning of procedures and policies that ensure good-quality products.

Quality circle: a group of between six and ten employees who volunteer to meet regularly to discuss work-related issues.

Quality control (QC): checking the product during the production run to test it against the specification.

Quantitative interviews: facts and brief answers are collected from the target market during face-to-face or telephone interviews.

Quick response manufacturing (QRM): the use of mainly computer-based technologies to manufacture small numbers of identical products efficiently and competitively.

Radar chart: a chart with a central point and radiating arms to display multiple sets of data on a single chart. Also known as a spider chart.

Raveled fabric: fabric that has yarn teased or drawn out from its cut edges giving it a frayed appearance.

Reasonably practicable: means balancing the level of risk against the measures needed to control the real risk in terms of money, time or trouble.

Regenerated fibre: a fibre made from natural cellulose that has been chemically modified.

Registered design: legal protection for a product's appearance or decoration to stop unauthorised copying.

Rendering: adding colour, shade, tone, texture to a drawing.

Repeating pattern: the distance between one point of a design and the exact point where it begins again.

Returnity: 100 per cent recyclable polyester fibres, used in clothing that is designed to be reused with zero waste.

Rip-proof/rip-stop fabric: has a distinctive woven-in raised square pattern that stops the fabric from ripping or tearing.

Risk assessment: a statutory process that considers what might cause harm to people and what reasonable steps might be taken to prevent that harm.

Rouleau loop: a thin tube of sewn and turned bias-cut fabric used to fasten dome-shaped buttons or frog fastenings.

Safety precautions: actions carried out in advance that protect against a possible danger or injury.

Secondary data: research collected from existing sources of data.

Self-finishing seam: raw edges of the seam are enclosed within the seam as it is constructed.

Slow fashion: durable fashionable garments that have a long product cycle.

Smart material: a material that is able to react to external stimuli or changes in its environment without human intervention.

Snagging: a defect in a textile product caused by pulling or plucking yarns from a fabric surface.

Socio-economic influences: the social and economic factors that help to shape lifestyle, attitudes and expectations.

Solvent: a chemical substance used to dissolve or dilute other substances or materials.

Specifications: used to test designs, prototypes and manufactured products.

Spinneret: the nozzle part of the spinning machine where the molten fibres are extruded.

Standard: an agreed and repeatable way of doing something, set out as a published document.

Sub-assembly: a self-contained, separately manufactured element incorporated in a final product's assembly.

Sustainability: the reduction of all aspects of design and manufacturing activity that have a negative impact on the environment or the lives of humans.

SWOT analysis: a process of evaluating the strengths, weaknesses, opportunities and threats of a business venture, project or product.

Synthetic fibre: a fibre made entirely from synthetic polymers based on petrochemicals.

Technical/modern materials: new materials that have been developed from their original form.

Template: a pattern used to transfer a design shape onto fabric to ensure accuracy in cutting.

Tex: the metric system used to state the thickness of a yarn.

Thermoplastic: a material that becomes soft and mouldable above a specific temperature and solidifies upon cooling.

Third-party feedback: objective observations from people not involved in the design, creation or promotion of the product.

Tolerance: the acceptable variation in the size of a product or part of a product, usually given as an upper and a lower limit.

Total quality management (TQM): a proactive approach followed by management and employees to ensure long-term customer satisfaction and loyalty.

Trade Descriptions Act (2011): makes it an offence for businesses to make false or misleading statements about goods or services.

Trademark: a unique combination of words, sounds, colours and logos used for marketing, and the legal protection of brand identity.

Trend forecasts: predictions for future fashions produced by forecasting businesses and sold to fashion design companies.

Unit production system (UPS): a computerised overhead transportation system that moves garment components automatically from one workstation to the next according to a pre-determined sequence.

Upcycle: to convert an unwanted piece of clothing or textile product into something useful and creative.

User-centred design (UCD): developing a new product to suit the needs and wants of the consumer.

Utility clothing: introduced by the British government during 1941 as an economic aid to conserve resources during the war years. Garment designs were modified to make them more efficient to produce.

Virtual prototype: a 3D prototype product modelled on a computer but not actually made.

Weight: the outcome of how a fabric has been woven, its finish and sometimes the fibre type.

With nap layout: all the paper pattern pieces must lie in the same direction on the fabric.

Xenon arc lamp: produces a bright white light that closely mimics natural sunlight.

Yarn: a long continuous length of twisted (spun) fibres used in the construction of woven and knitted fabrics.